THE FOUNDATIONS OF PSYCHOANALYTIC THEORIES

THE FOUNDATIONS OF PSYCHOANALYTIC THEORIES

Project for a Scientific Enough Psychoanalysis

Vesa Talvitie

KARNAC

First published in 2012 by
Karnac Books Ltd
118 Finchley Road
London NW3 5HT

British Library Cataloguing in Publication Data

A C.I.P. for this book is available from the British Library

ISBN-13: 978-1-85575-817-9

Typeset by Vikatan Publishing Solutions (P) Ltd., Chennai, India

Printed in Great Britain

www.karnacbooks.com

CONTENTS

ACKNOWLEDGEMENTS

Writing a book contains extremely positive social and intellectual side effects: such a project offers an excellent reason for conversations and debates with colleagues. In the discussions around one or several chapters of this book the following people have presented interesting and valuable comments: Simon Boag, Henrik Enckell, Erkki Heinonen, Juhani Ihanus, Rauno Juntumaa, Jussi Kotkavirta, Anssi Peräkylä, Panu Varjonen, and especially Tuomas Valsta. I hope that in the future these people will again offer me plenty of opportunities to participate in such discussions as a commentator. Special thanks to Olli Sarmaja for the cover picture.

ABOUT THE AUTHOR

Vesa Talvitie is a Doctor of Psychology, licensed psychotherapist, and organisational consultant (FINOD). He currently works as an occupational psychologist for the City of Helsinki. He is the author of the book *The Freudian Unconscious and Cognitive Neuroscience: From Unconscious Fantasies to Neural Algorithms* (2009, Karnac) and of several articles in English and Finnish. His articles on psychoanalysis (with Juhani Ihanus) have been published in *The International Journal of Psychoanalysis* and *Neuro-Psychoanalysis*, among others. For further information, visit his homepage www.vesatalvitie.fi.

INTRODUCTION

The title of this publication paraphrases Sigmund Freud's work "Project for a scientific psychology" (1895), written more than a century ago. Debates around psychoanalysis are almost as old as that writing of Freud, and thus the aim of this book is rather bold: to say something fresh about the scientific status of psychoanalysis, and set the discipline into the frames that are plausible from the viewpoints of both clinical practice and present-day academic study.

When it is talked about the foundations of psychoanalysis, reference is normally being made to Freud's notions and ideas when creating the discipline. In this book, however, I will focus on foundations of a different kind—the ones that psychoanalysis shares with all branches of the behavioural sciences. Consequently, in the following chapters psychoanalytic theories and models will be approached through certain grand themes of psychology and neuroscience.

Views concerning psychoanalysis are probably more diverged than any other discipline. On one side there are advocates of psychoanalysis. Clinicians, psychoanalysts, and psychotherapists form the majority of this group, but it is made up also of more and less educated lay people, artists, and humanist researchers. Some respected scientists—let us make mention of the Nobel Prize winners Gerald Edelman and Eric

Kandel here—have also expressed sympathies towards psychoanalysis. On the opposite side we find "Freud-bashers" and a group of serious critics: the philosophers Frank Cioffi, Ernest Gellner, Adolf Grünbaum, and Karl Popper; the converts Frederic Crews, Jeffrey Masson, and Alice Miller; the historian Paul Roazen …

In this polarised situation it is difficult to appear as just curiously studying psychoanalytic topics in the present-day academic and clinical contexts; and I would like to see this book as an invitation for both camps to look at psychoanalysis differently.

Freud described the mind/brain as a hydraulic machine, and later cognitive science treated it in terms of a digital machine, a computer. A machine-metaphor can also be applied to depict the production of academic writings. Some weeks ago I met an old friend of mine who is a neuroscientist. He reacted to my "How is it going?" question, by telling me that "The machine still works well": last year my friend and his collaborator had published more than ten articles. I liked to see the process that lead to my thesis and the book *The Freudian Unconscious and Cognitive Neuroscience: From Unconscious Fantasies to Neural Algorithms* (Talvitie, 2009) as a rather mechanical act of translation: take a "psychoanalytic" phenomena, and just describe it by using the terms of cognitive neuroscience. I thought as if there where a machine in my head, in which I may put psychoanalytic stuff (phenomena, notions, theories …). As a result of my (and my collaborators' Juhani Ihanus' and Hannu Tiitinen's) cognitive process there came out interdisciplinary writings, published in scientific journals.

The machine-metaphor works even better with Freud's writings. After having developed the basic building-blocks of psychoanalysis—the ideas concerning the unconscious, sexuality, and defences, and the structural model—Freud was able to apply his viewpoint to a wide spectre of phenomena: psychic disorders, jokes, dreams, paintings, slips of the tongue, novels, perversions, and so on. Before introducing the "machine" that produced this book, let us put forward some notions concerning the battleground around psychoanalysis.

Perhaps the majority of both critics and advocates rely on a certain conception of psychoanalysis as a theory. According to this understanding, at the core of psychoanalysis there are claims—true or erroneous—on the causes of disorders and human behaviour. Critics state that the claims are erroneous or those made cannot be empirically studied, and the advocates argue the contrary. Quite often the latter also suggest that psychoanalysis is an extraordinary scientific discipline that cannot be appraised by using the conventional criteria of science.

The above conception may be seen as emerging from a certain orientation concerning the philosophy of science. It may be said to be "empiricistic", or possessing echoes from "positivism" or "logical empiricism". These (rather bad-sounding) terms are not the crucial matter, however. The above conception should be studied in the light of certain more recent trends of the philosophy of science. More importantly, it is alien for the field of which psychoanalysis is a part. Namely, as I will argue, with that conception one cannot make sense of psychoanalysis, or other branches of psychotherapy, or the clinical practice of psychiatry.

Researchers' machines normally consist of a mixture of scientific terms, empirical observations, and theories or models. Freud built his particular machine himself. Contrary to that, I'm leaning on two pre-existing (current) views: those concerning the essence of psychology and psychological theories in general, and those concerning the philosophy of science.

When it comes to the first viewpoint, it is obvious that psychoanalysis is a psychologial discipline. However, what has not been recognised is the importance of the question: "What kind of psychology is psychoanalysis?" The question is rather tricky since psychology is a very diverse discipline—the American Psychological Association (APA) has more than fifty divisions, and the branches of psychology possess neither a shared methodological nor theoretical basis. When approaching different psychological issues, such as the age for children to start school, the factors behind high blood pressure, which kind of television advertisements are most effective, or how to cure idiosynchratic psychic disorders in psychotherapy, it is clear that different methods of study are needed and are available. Neither should it be news that the criteria for a scientific psychological theory vary. I will show in the following chapters that, for example, Adolf Grünbaum's critique is based on a particular conception of psychology that has not been advocated in the scientific community for decades.

Since psychoanalysis is not an island in the sea of science, I will introduce several general issues concerning the essence of psychology, and embed specific psychoanalytic topics into them: To what do psychological terms make reference?; Can psychological models and theories present reasons for and/or causes of human behaviour?; What are psychological explanations like?; Which matters can be called "mental", and on what basis?; and How should idiosynchratic phenomena (that psychoanalysis is interested in) be studied in the scope of science and humanities? I believe it is clear even from the outset that studying psychoanalytic issues from this kind of viewpoint is fruitful.

The second component of my machine treats issues falling in the domain of the philosophy of science. In terms of the topic of this book, the core questions of that discipline are the following: What makes the difference between "science" and "non-science"?; Can the scientific method be determined?; Is there a common scientific method for all branches of study?; and Should humanistic study try to mirror that of the natural sciences? When these questions are applied in the context of psychoanalysis, they become transformed to slightly more concrete questions: On what basis might one state that psychoanalysis is or is not a scientific discipline?; and Can neuroscience be of help when determining the scientific status of psychoanalysis?

The "philosophy of psychology" and the "philosophy of science" may sound abstract, and the above considerations may make the reader anticipate a rather burdensome experience of reading. The topic at hand is challenging, and this book does not fall into the "Psychoanalysis for Dummies" or "What Freud really said" genres. However, the branches of philosophy are not academic nerds' playgrounds, in which focus is placed on insignificant matters. If, for instance, the plausibility of the Freudian idea of the "Oedipus complex" is studied, the considerations remain superficial if one does not take into account the above "philosophical" perspectives and ask questions such as "Is psychology in general able to present universal laws?" and "Which kind of matters does the (psychological) term 'Oedipus complex' actually refer to?" I swear that the book at hand is at least much more accessible than its predecessor, Freud's "Project" (1895).

In Freud's lifetime the classics of philosophy such as Hegel and Kant were still appreciated, and positivism had its heyday. It is not news that the current spirit in the philosophy of science is very different. Much has happened also after the most well-known critiques of psychoanalysis—Karl Popper's critique in the 1930s that psychoanalytic claims cannot be falsified, and Adolf Grünbaum's first critical articles of psychoanalysis in the 1970s. Both present-day advocates and critics of psychoanalysis tend to ignore the recent views of the philosophy of science. The picture the critics have painted, by leaning on Freud's hundred-year-old writings, may have been appropriate fifty years ago, but currently it is a straw-man from the point of view of both psychodynamic clinicians (a topic to which I will return at the end of the section) and the philosophers of science.

When studying these matters in the following chapters we will, of course, direct attention also to neuropsychoanalysis, often considered as the most up-to-date conception of psychoanalysis. Freud characterises his "Project" by stating: "The intention is to furnish a psychology that shall be a natural science" (Freud, 1895, p. 295), and that spirit is alive also in the domain of neuropsychoanalysis. Neuropsychoanalysis has shown remarkable disregard towards studies concerning the essence of psychology and the relation between psychology and neuroscience (a topic which falls into the domains of the philosophy of science and the philosophy of mind). Due to these shortcomings, neuropsychoanalysis has not been able to present a well-articulated rationale on how neuroscientific studies might help to develop better psychoanalytic theories. Thus its foundations have remained extremely confused (Talvitie & Ihanus, 2011a; Talvitie & Ihanus, 2011b).

The idea that the theories of a clinical discipline—for example, whatever school of psychotherapy or psychiatry—might present (psychological) laws, be based mainly in empirical research, and will mirror the theories of natural science, is very strange from the perspectives of both present-day psychiatry (for example, Kendler & Parnas, 2008; Murphy, 2009; Zachar, 2000) and the philosophy of science (Godfrey-Smith, 2003; van Frassen, 2008; Wimsatt, 2007). Reductionism is currently rarely advocated, and the mainstream philosophy of science holds that the criteria of science vary depending on the particular discipline in question.

Needless to mention, this does not imply that the psychoanalytic community (no more than, say, the communities of the astrologists or anthroposophists) might tailor suitable criteria for scientificity as it likes. However, as will be seen, more recent ideas of the philosophy of science enable us to make sense of the nature of the psychoanalytic affair, and free ourselves from the saps of the age-old Freud wars.

Let us make here the notion that those Freud wars have taken place in some kind of vacuum. As far as the scientific status of psychoanalysis appears as some kind of problem, in many, or even most, cases, the same problem concerns also other branches of psychotherapy. But has anybody seen debates on whether cognitive psychotherapy (or some of its branches) or family therapy is science? Behind the title of the book there is the idea that no branch of psychotherapy is a science, and thus one should only be concerned as to whether the branch under consideration is scientific *enough*.

It might be said that in the following chapters I will decompose and reassemble the Freudian machine by using my own two-component machine. This, of course, implies that the same can be done to *my* machine. It would be naïve to think of oneself as presenting some kind of final account of the topic at hand, and thus I have a more modest hope: being able to reformulate the discussion around psychoanalysis. My hope is that when someone disagrees with my view (from the pro or the con position), the disagreement is rather easy to formulate in an accessible manner. Namely, a critic can easily tell which part(s) of my machine his or her disagreement concerns: what psychology in general, or psychoanalysis in particular, is (or should be) like; or the criteria for well-founded beliefs in a particular topic (the philosophy of science). This kind of frame, which enables location of the disagreement to a more general academic context, also is of help in formulating a rival view.

Present-day psychoanalysis contains several branches, and when someone is talking about psychoanalysis, it is always accurate to present the question "Which psychoanalysis?" (see, for example, Stepansky, 2009). In order to present a comprehensive image of even just mainstream psychoanalysis, one should introduce at least Freudian (whatever it means), Lacanian, Kohutian, and Jungian psychoanalysis, the American ego-psychology, and the British object-relations school. More recent mentalisation-based views should not be left out either. Such a study might lead to a conclusion that there is no such a thing as psychoanalysis, but rather many psychoanalytically oriented traditions.

In this work this tension is managed by focusing on the issues that the majority of the psychoanalytic community recognises as belonging at the core of the discipline. I think that at the core we find five matters: Freud's structural model (thinking in terms of the id, the ego, and the super-ego); the presupposition of the mental unconscious; approaching behaviour and mental operations in terms of defences and transference; the importance of sexuality; and interest towards the historical (developmental) aspect of disorders and personality traits (see Westen, 1998).

We must ask whether the majority of psychodynamic folks really accept these matters, and if there are other matters that should be counted as belonging in the core. When it comes to the former question, I believe it is difficult to find a psychoanalytically oriented rersearcher or clinician who does not feel at home with these five topics. Concerning the rival core elements of the above five, I think that there are no evident candidates. For example, Freud's "metapsychology", Melanie Klein's "paranoid-schizoid position", Heinz Hartman's "ego's conflict-free sphere", and C. G. Jung's "collective unconscious", possess either marginal or very controversial status in the psychoanalytic community. I'm afraid that if one does not accept the above five basic building-blocks as characterising psychoanalysis, it is not possible to treat psychoanalysis as a whole.

There is also an additional challenge when aiming at creating an appropriate big picture of psychoanalysis. Namely, we get one image of psychoanalysis by reading psychoanalytic texts, the old and recent writings in books and psychoanalytic journals, but quite a different one when talking with clinicians. Only a minority of psychodynamists ever publish, and it is worth asking how well the writers represent the views of the psychoanalytic folks. It might be claimed that in "official" writings psychoanalysis appears as more theoretical, more different from some other forms of psychotherapy, as well as more Freudian and rigid than in the minds and conversations of average clinicians (see, for example, Sandler, 1983; Westen, 1998, p. 335). It has been claimed that "what psychoanalytic psychotherapists do is rather better than what they write" (Frosh, 1997, p. 42). Thus there is a danger that academic debates on psychoanalysis take place around a straw-man, who does not exist in (clinical) reality.

The output of my mental machine is organised around two core questions: "What is the essence of psychology and psychoanalysis?", and "What is their relation to neuroscience?" In the first two chapters it is studied the essence of psychoanalytic and other psychological *concepts*, and their characteristics in relation to neurobiological ones. The third chapter approaches psychology and neuroscience from the perspective of *explanations* that they provide. The fourth chapter—written together with Juhani Ihanus, basing on the article having been published in *The Scandinavian Psychoanalytic Review* (Talvitie & Ihanus, 2011a), and reproduced here with the kind permission of the publisher—takes psychological and neurobiological *mechanisms* under scrutiny. Chapter five concerns metaphysics, and before the concluding chapter we focus on the psychoanalytic view of words denoting objects, and how that possesses considerable implications for the scientific status of psychoanalytic theories.

The seven chapters do form a continuum. However, they stand as independent entities to the extent that a reader should feel free to create a reading-order reflecting his or her own interests.

CHAPTER ONE

Psychoanalysis and its concepts I: on the essence of psychological concepts

Why do the terms of other branches of behavioural science not suffice for psychoanalysis, meaning that specific psychoanalytic concepts are needed? The answer is probably related to the notion that every psychological theory should recognise the essence of the human (or at least a certain aspect of it). Supposedly in the human there are strivings, instincts, feelings, mental images, behavioural dispositions, representations, and different kinds of mental and neural states and processes. If a psychological theory is plausible, it—among other things—has labels and concepts for those matters. On this basis one might state that the existence of specific psychoanalytic terms reflects the fact that psychoanalysis has recognised aspects of human essence that still remain neglected or unnoticed by other branches of the behavioural sciences.

This kind of straightforward claim is an "Alexandrian solution" (to the Gordian Knot) giving rise to opposite claims in a similar spirit. (An opponent may state that psychoanalysis actually projects imaginary matters into man.) Below I begin developing a more sophisticated conception to the Tower of Babel dilemma.

The language of psychoanalysis

Clear terminology cannot be counted among the strengths of psychoanalysis. Laplanche and Pontalis' *The Language of Psychoanalysis* (1973) is the classical dictionary of psychoanalysis, and in its introduction Daniel Lagache states: "Aversion to psycho-analysis sometimes takes the form of disparaging comments about its terminology. Naturally, psycho-analysts do not endorse the abuse or overhasty use of technical words as a way of covering up woolly thinking" (Lagache, 1973, p. vii). *The Language of Psychoanalysis,* first published in 1967 (in French), focused on Freud's work and contained 300 terms. Salman Akhtar's *Comprehensive Dictionary of Psychoanalysis* appeared in 2009. As its name indicates, the book is more comprehensive with 1,800 entries. In the Introduction, Akhtar (2009, p. xi) describes the making of the dictionary in an entertaining manner. He states that the purpose of the book is "to create a civilized order out of a delicious chaos".

But why such a "chaos"? It probably has something to do with the existence of several "languages" (or vocabularies), which psychoanalysis has to cope with. First, there are several languages inside psychoanalysis. The relations between psychoanalytic schools are complicated, sometimes even hostile, and this gives rise to several questions: Is (just) one of those psychoanalytic theories true, or would it be possible that they all were true, either partly or in full? Could we perhaps take the best parts of each of them? If we could, who would tell us the best parts, and on what basis?

Second, there is the need to determine the relation between psychoanalytic terminology and the terminology used in the academic world. There are terms—for example, "representation", "instinct", and "defence"—that are used both in the domain of psychoanalysis and outside it. With such words there is the question of whether they possess the same meaning in psychoanalytic contexts as they do in others, or if the psychoanalytic use of the term contains a specific psychoanalytic subtlety (when the same terms are used by different "psychoanalytic dialects", there is also the possibility that they are actually homonyms). As mentioned, it is rather drastic to claim that psychoanalytic terms not used by other disciplines reflects the superiority of psychoanalysis (and the narrow-mindedness of others). The dilemma around the Tower of Babel becomes more relaxed when we deteminine on a general level the possible points of reference of psychological terms.

To what do psychological concepts refer?

It is certainly unsatisfactory to simply state that psychological concepts refer to the mind or psyche—there are lots of psychological concepts, and their reference points are diverse. When thinking of psychoanalytic and psychological terms in general, we find three main categories:

- *Phenomenal matters that appear in the domain of consciousness.* Let us mention as examples mental images, stream of consciousness, the sensation of smell, a feeling of pain, and a feeling of anxiety.
- *Entities or "things" that are supposed to exist in the mind or brain.* One may claim that the mind or brain contains, for example, mental apparatus, memory traces, the ego, an executive control system, unconscious fantasies, schemata, and censorship. In many cases one can—or perhaps even should—present the question of whether the term really refers to an existing entity or if it is a construct.
- *Constructions.*
  a. *Constructions of entities and processes.* Nobody thinks that we might pinpoint from the mind or the brain (or anywhere else) a self-image or feeling of self-esteem (high or low), and I believe that only a few think that we have schemata on behaving in restaurants in our heads. Such terms are constructs that draw together many matters on how a person feels, thinks, behaves, and interprets matters around him- or herself.

     There is a long list of psychoanalytic concepts where the point of reference is a difficult one to show or determine, and there should be disputes on whether they fall into the category of constructions or that of existing entities: primary process, censorship, mental unconscious, repressed desire, the id, mental apparatus, and so on.

  b. *Constructions of behavioural and affective-cognitive dispositions.* When a person is suggested to be, for example, ambitious, an extrovert, representing the type A behaviour pattern, or using a certain information-processing strategy, it is claimed that his or her behaviour is characterised by a certain pattern of reacting and behaving—one often, but not always, acts or reacts in a certain way.

     The psychoanalytic terms "defensive", "intellectualising", "poor impulse control", and "depressive position", fall into this category. Let us stress that calling, for example, "poor impulse control", a construct, does not mean that one doubts that the person in question gets temper tantrums—"construct" is not a pejorative term.

c. *Constructions of one's relation to another person, and the type of interaction with two people.* The concepts "symbiosis" (symbiotic) and "projective identification" are examples of concepts in this category.
d. *Constructions of a developmental stage and phase.* Freud, Erik Erikson, and Jean Piaget prominently have created theories in which developmental stages enjoy a significant role. Piaget's "pre-operational" and Freud's "oral stage" are perhaps the best-known representatives of the terms of this category.

Psychological concepts of the first two categories—phenomenal matters, and entities or "things" that are supposed to exist in the mind/brain—are correct or erroneous simply in terms of whether or not the phenomenon or entity they refer to exists. Constructs, the third category, abstract or conceptualise behavioural patterns and mental matters. Thus, we should evaluate constructs only in terms of how useful and exact they are—a good concept is defined in an unambiguous manner, and it pinpoints a (rather) well-defined phenomenon. As a part of a theory, good constructs may neverthleless enable us to explain matters: if we find a strong correlation between, for example, low self-esteem and a particular psychic disorder, we have a partial explanation of a phenomenon.

When studying whatever approach or theory, psychoanalytic or other, it is not a bad idea to start with terminology: which of the categories different concepts fall into. When the cognitivist tradition is under scrutiny, it is to be determined whether or not, for example, a schemata, memory-traces, and the executive control system, are supposed to be constructs or existing entities of the mind/brain. Similarly, in the case of psychoanalysis, it should be made clear whether the terms "ego", "censorship", "the unconscious", "defence mechanism", "unconscious fantasy", "repression", and "projective identification" are considered as constructs or if they are held to refer to entities or processes that can be pinpointed.

As a preliminary notion, we can state that when there are disagreements as to whether certain concepts are constructs, or if the concepts refer to existing entities, one deals with serious, metaphysical disagreements (see Chapter Two and Chapter Five). With concepts that are seen as constructs, the situation is radically different: since traditions of research possess different interests, it is extremely natural (and actually unavoidable) that they construct their objects of study differently (an issue approached especially in Chapter Three). In the following section we take a look at the hard core of academic psychology, and my aim is to show that most, if not all, psychological concepts should be seen as constructs.

On the constructive nature of the concepts of academic psychology

In his book *How to Think Straight about Psychology*, Keith Stanovich (2010) approaches the essence of academic, empirical psychology, and characterises psychology through nine statements (p. 206). When studying the essence of psychoanalytic psychology, it is illuminating to take a look at his views.

Some of Stanovich's theses describe science in general: data and theories are presented in the public domain; knowledge is acquired after slow accumulation of data; there is methodological pluralism. The thesis concerning falsifiable theories is common to psychoanalytic folks from Popper's critique, and when treating the demand on systematic empiricism, Stanovich criticises psychoanalysis in a similar manner to how many of his colleagues have done.

He also states that psychology investigates *solvable problems*. This means that psychology should keep a distance from metaphysical topics and leave them to philosophers. Stanovich himself is very restricted with this issue: from the book we do not find a definition of "psyche" or the writer's view on the essence of it, and Stanovich does not even mention the mind–body problem. Regardless, the thesis concerning solvable problems should be noted in psychoanalytic circles, too. Namely, Freud is occasionally thought to have solved the problem concerning the relation between psyche and soma (the mind–body problem), and such claims bring psychoanalytic theories into the domain of philosophy. That leads to a difficult multi-front battle.

Stanovich (2010, pp. 35–52) stresses that psychological concepts are constructs. For example, the type A behaviour pattern consists of the following elements: a strong desire to compete; a potential for hostility; time-urgent behaviour; and an intense drive to accomplish goals.

He states that even psychological concepts such as "depression", "anxiety", "attachment", and "aggression" are constructs having different meanings in scientific discourse and in everyday language. Bem and Looren de Jong put it as follows: "Take for instance attitude, role, belief, the unconscious, whatever. It is hardly possible to restrict the connotations these terms have in daily life, and give unambiguous scientific definitions, without loss of meaning or without changing them beyond recognition" (Bem & Looren de Jong, 2006, p. 31).

Let us make some notions on the Big Five model of personality, one of the great theories of psychology. The first step in the formulation of the model was taken when Gordon Allport and H. S. Odpert took a look at the English dictionary in the 1930s, and listed 18,000 personality-related expressions. A decade later, Cattell formed a list of 171 expressions most commonly used when describing other people, reduced them to less than 40 clusters, and through factor analysis to 12 variables. Later, through the work of Fiske, Tupes, and Christal the factors were still reduced to five. The factors of the Big Five are Extraversion; Agreeableness (Warmth); Conscientiousness; Emotional stability (neuroticism); and Intellectance (openness to experience). (McAdams, 1992)

Thus, the Big Five model did not begin with scientific observations on what the human being is like, but on how we use language in our daily life. Through statistical methods, researchers determined the bunch of traits that described the aspects of the human in as both an economical and as comprehensive a manner as possible. The Big Five theorists argue that those five traits represent people's enduring, distinctive dispositional tendencies, and the model has been found to be able to predict, for example, political preferences. It has to be noted that the model focuses on people's *average* tendencies, and there has been little interest towards the psychological mechanisms behind the factors and traits.

"Personality traits" are closely related to the goals of people's actions. Research on "temperament" reflects a different interest—the focus is on the qualities of human acts and mentation. Both trait theories and those concerned with temperament lack sensitivity towards the significance of the context, since their interest is elsewhere: they aim to sketch people's average tendencies and behavioural disposition on the level of population. Researchers' claims with respect to different kinds of temperaments and traits are constructs in particular, and it is difficult to see how they might *explain* humans' behaviour in the strict sense of that word. (Boag, 2011; Caprara & Cervone, 2000, pp. 62–84)

It seems that non-psychoanalytic psychological concepts are used as constructs, and that leads us to ask whether psychoanalytic concepts are exceptional in this respect. I will not give an answer—or my proposal to such—here. Instead, I am contented with elaborating the notion made above: it is very unlikely that the concepts that are held to be constructs, would become as serious obstacles for interdisciplinary research or for the scientific status of psychoanalysis. Or, the other way round: it is better to be careful and minimalistic when postulating entities into the mind/brain.

In daily situations—in the roles of psychotherapists as well as their clients, among others—we use so-called "folk-psychology". We get a different perspective to the essence of psychoanalytic terminology by studying it in terms of its relation to that everyday psychological vocabulary.

Folk-psychology, scientific psychology, and psychotherapy

Stanovich stresses the difference between the language and essence of scientific psychology on the one hand, and lay-person psychology on the other. This issue makes a difference between psychotherapists and academic researchers: psychotherapy is bound to folk-psychology, since psychotherapists have to be able to convert their theoretical ideas to the everyday language.

We do not know exactly when our ancestors became folk-psychologists. Homerian poems, the earliest extant literature from the seventh century B.C., contain folk-psychology that is familiar to present-day people: people are driven by passions, fears, and inner dramas. Folk-psychologies of different times and cultures possess idiosynchratic characteristics, and, for example, the vocabularies for mental matters vary. However, it is not necessary to go into such details here. For us the crucial thing is the intimate relationship between lay-person psychology and our self-understanding: we make sense of ourselves through (the terms of) folk-psychology in particular. To put the essence of folk-psychology in a formal manner, philosophers of mind hold that folk-psychology is comprised of so-called *propositional attitudes*. This expression refers to statements like "X remembers that …"; "X desires that …"; "X believes that …"; and "X fears that …"—folk-psychology is often characterised as presupposing that we have "sentences in the head".

Philosophers have also taken notice of the astonishing predictive power of folk-psychology. Actually, no discipline is more dependent on lay-person ideas—"pre-scientific" conceptions—than psychology, and the power of folk-psychology and its relation to academic psychology has been a challenging puzzle. There is vast literature on the topic, and, for example, Charter and Oaksford's (1996), Smith's (1996), Place's (1996), Richard's (1996), and Valentine's (1996) essays in the book *The Philosophy of Psychology* (edited by O'Donohue and Kitchener) represent the range of diverging views.

In order to illustrate the power of folk-psychology, let us suppose that one is acquainted with David, and knows that he will go to a Congress held in Copenhagen by aeroplane on Monday morning. When these matters are set in the context of folk-psychology, we get the following presupposition: David *wants* to participate in the Congress; he *knows* how to get there by aeroplane; he *knows* that one has to arrive at the airport on time to catch the flight; he hates hasty situations, etc. On this basis one is able to make the astonishing prediction that on Monday David will wake up early, dabble with his suitcase, and order a taxi.

Psychological issues are a pervasive and self-evident part of our daily activities, and yet for much of the time we operate unaware of our folk-psychological ideas and lines of thought. Thus, the above considerations on folk-psychology may sound trivial. However, the crucial thing is that when predicting human behaviour, in many cases folk-psychology beats scientific psychology by far—no academic psychological or other theory is able to predict people's behaviour that way. The modern equipment of neuroscientists may tell whether one thinks of a square or a circle, but they cannot tell that David will meet Alan next Friday in Harry's pub, or that next Monday he will go to the airport.

Physicists may turn up their noses at folk-physics, but psychologists cannot do the same with folk-psychology. Folk-psychology possesses remarkable predictive power, and also lays the conceptual basis for scientific psychology. Namely, scientific papers are full of folk-psychological vocabulary, that is, talk about beliefs, knowledge, memory, and desires. Folk-psychology is simply inevitable: our daily activities, for example, contracts made between a therapist and a client, as well as legal processes, are based on it. All schools of psychotherapies lean on folk-psychology, and indeed it it is hard to even conceive a form of psychotherapy that would not—it is difficult to talk and think about personal matters in terms other than that of folk-psychology.

We all understand what "I know that Paris is the capital of France" and "I want coffee" mean, but it is another thing to tell how our knowledge, fears, and desires exist in our minds—an issue extremely crucial for the topic at hand. As far as we cannot tell the mental and/or neural state of things that sentences such as "Lester desires his boss's wife" and "Earl fears he will be fired" refer to, we can neither tell what *repressed* desires and fears are. In the rather long section below I focus on this issue and show why our *beliefs, desires, and fears should be considered as constructs*. Chapter Six contains my suggestion as to how becoming conscious of the repressed should be understood on this basis.

Existence of knowledge, memory, fear, and desire

We must begin with an odd-sounding question: On what basis do we know that humans possess desires, memories, and knowledge? The answer is simply either taking seriously what people say ("Yes, *I know* that the aeroplane to Copenhagen leaves at seven o'clock"; "Yes, *I desire* having a lower handicap in golf"), that is, the first person point-of-view, or observing people's behaviour (noticing the early awakening, and the practising of the golf swing), that is, the third person point-of-view. Formally speaking, the problem is why people behave as they do and say such things, and the answer is: because they possess desires, beliefs, and knowledge.

But where do desires, beliefs, and pieces of knowledge exist, and what do they "look like"?—actually they cannot exist as "sentences in the head". When considering the first person point-of-view proof of their existence, one might state that they exist in our consciousness: I know that Paris is the capital of France and that I desire to have a lower handicap because I have the feelings of knowing and desiring. But how about when thinking of other things (as I mainly do): Where are the pieces of knowledge and desires? The answer "in my mind" is insufficient: Where exactly is a memory when it is said to be in the mind?

The problem becomes more striking when we think of, for example, the question: Is the town Kilkenny (of Ireland) north or south from Finland? Even if Kilkenny would become associated only to bier, it is possible to give a correct answer: one "knows", basing on general knowledge concerning geography, that Kilkenny is south from Finland. Thus, we must think that a bigger or smaller part of our knowledge does not (pre-)exist in our head; it is *generated in the situation at hand through reasoning*.

There are additional problems with the idea that our knowledge and desires could somehow be pinpointed, and that they would be accessible to introspection. Consider saying to David, "I see that you are going to the airport. Do you desire to reach the aeroplane, go to the conference or to become informed on the latest news of your discipline?" He might respond: "Eh? All those things, I assume ..." In other words, our goals form a hiearchy. Perhaps it is better not to think that David's behaviour is motivated by one particular desire. Instead, we might think that he (as well as other people) verbalises (constructs) his desire differently depending on the context, and there is no single "objective" description of the desire.

It has to also be borne in mind that stating "I desire/know/ remember this-and-this" is sometimes just a habit of talk. If it is asked, "Do you practice golf in order to play the rounds faster?", one may say, "No, that's not the point at all". However, the question nevertheless makes some weird sense, and with a positive answer one can avoid more lengthy discussion with a person having no idea on golf.

The other way to induce that someone is having or recalling a desire/ memory/piece of knowedge was by observing a person's behaviour (from the third person point-of-view). This way appears as even more arbitrary: the observer projects into the person's mind/brain matters having him- or herself incorporated from folk-psychology of the surrounding culture or scientific psychology.

In the domain of cognitive orientation, the problems treated above are studied under the heading *knowledge representation*. The researchers of the field see the basic picture as follows (see, for example, Audi, 1998, pp. 74–91; Squire & Kandel, 1999).

There are several memory-systems. Recall of events reflects the functioning of episodic memory. The brain contains memory-traces of past events, which may become activated when one tries to recall the event or when an appropriate stimulus is perceived. Memory-traces represent events only fragmentarily, and a successful memory-performance presumes several neural and mental processess. All present-day researchers of memory stress that in the mind or brain there is no cabinet from which memories are retrieved. Instead, remembering is a constructive process in particular. Thus, memories do not exist ready-made in our heads, but they become constructed through several neural and conscious processes.

Knowledge falls in the domain of semantic memory. Our brain codes facts as "chunks", and similarly as with episodic memory, memory-performances are outcomes of several entangled processes.

Semantic and episodic memory are commonly characterised as reflecting "know *that* ..." knowledge. There are also non-conscious forms of knowledge and memories; for example, there are different kinds of skills involving *to know how*. Several paradigms of research study those non-conscious forms of memory and knowledge, and thus it is talked about implicit memory, tacit knowledge, and procedural knowledge. I have elsewhere (Talvitie & Ihanus, 2002) treated this topic more extensively, and it is not necessary to go into details here. Thus, let us turn to study desires and fears.

Desires (and the same holds for fears) should be thought to possess, first, a cognitive or a representative aspect: in order to desire (or fear), one has to know different matters about the object of desire. This aspect falls in the domain of knowledge-representation. Second, they possess an executive aspect, which is more difficult to approach: How do the powers or forces that make us act in a, for example, sexual, aggressive, or altruistic manner, exist? One dimension of the trouble with desires relates to the mind–body problem. Namely, it is a mystery how the mind, lacking extensions, is able to affect the body causally. Even without that mystery, pinpointing powers or forces is a difficult affair (Hacker, 2010, pp. 90–121).

Consider the powers of champagne to pop up the cap when the bottle is shaken, a steam or combustion engine to move a train, and dynamite to cause an explosion. In these examples the power may be located somewhere (champagne, the engine, steam, gasoline, dynamite), but there are several conditions (pressure, heat, fire) that the actualisation of the power necessitates. Thus, in these examples the power is not a thing, a single entity or force that might be pinpointed.

Determining and locating forces and powers seems to be difficult even in the physical world. Thus, even if the mind/brain were a steam-engine, the executive aspect of desires (and fears) could neither be reduced to a thing, a substance, stuff, or a certain part of it: terms such as "fear" and "desire" reflect complicated non-linear dynamics between different kinds of neural and mental matters, and between representational and executive aspects.

We might say (in the Wittgensteinian spirit) that folk-psychology is less about the real entities and processes of the mind/brain, and more a tool for social interaction: it has developed in order to make possible the ability to predict and affect the behaviour of others. The philosophers' thought-experiment called "inverted spectrum" illustrates how words are tied to social interaction.

At the heart of the thought-experiment is the question "How do we know that red as it appears to me is similar to your red?" Namely, in principle it would be possible that you see red as you see it, but red surfaces appear to me similarly as, say, green ones to you. As far as the appearances of colours are constant—your red is always red, and my red is always green—discussions about colours do not lead to open controversities.

In daily life people sometimes have disagreements on which colours fit together, say in items of fashion, and actually it would make sense to think that it is because colours appear differently to different persons. Thus, the moral of the inverted-spectrum thought-experiment is that although we fluently make use of psychological concepts (researchers of vision would swear that colours are psychological concepts) in daily interaction, this does not prove that people are making reference to similar experiences when using them.

A non-philosopher may be suspicious towards the inverted-spectrum thought-experiment. But let us think about other psychological concepts such as "envy" and "love". Would a psychoanalysed neurotic on the one hand, and a person who Otto Kernberg used to call "a borderline personality", on the other, refer to the same matters when using those words? Both are able to use the terms "correctly" in daily interaction, but I would claim that that does not prove the same reference point. Namely, a psychoanalysed neurotic has spent several hours in (painful) reflection of those words, but a borderline personality cannot tolerate the feeling of envy, and his or her love may turn suddenly to hate. Thus, love and envy really mean different matters to them. This state of things strengthens the claim that the concepts of folk-psychology—that form the foundations of both all psychotherapies and academic psychology—do not refer to entities of the mind/brain, but are rather constructs and habits of talk.

To conclude, on the one hand, desires, fears, and knowledge as propositional attitudes ("P desires/fears/knows X") form a foundation for humans' self-understanding and social interaction, and thus it is difficult to put them seriously under question. On the other hand, the mind/brain does not contain such propositional attitudes, and thus behavioural sciences have troubles in determining their relation to those powerful tools of folk-psychology. We can formulate this situation by stating that, on the one side, the concepts of folk-psychology refer to our mind/brain, but on the the other, they are strongly shaped by the surrounding culture—its vocabulary and habits of talk, and the pressure to cope with daily social interactions.

Concluding remark: the essentialist and nominalist views towards psychological concepts

The above considerations can be tightened to two different views concerning the essence of psychological concepts. According to the "essentialistic" view, a concept is plausible only if it refers to an existing entity. Thus, we are justified to talk about "schemata", "primary process", "ego", and "psychic tension" only if we are able to show, measure, and pinpoint the entity that the term in question is supposed to refer to. Advocating an essentialist position means that one denies the value of psychological concepts that are constructs. This denial makes the essentialistic position difficult to defend, since there are surely useful psychological concepts that are constructs. Thus, perhaps nobody is willing to defend a strict essentialist view.

Let us call the other position "nominalistic". A nominalist admits that psychological terms are constructs, and thus he or she accepts talk about, for example, super-egos or catharsis on the basis that the concepts may enable a psychotherapist to understand their clients and make better interventions. Usefulness of a construct depends on one's interest, and thus, for example, a psychotherapist and a consultant recruiting staff for companies may use different terms. In a nominalist's world there are an infinite number of potentially fruitful constructs.

The nominalist position has its problems. If psychological concepts are only constructs, and if we think that a construct is acceptable as long as it works, we would find ourselves in the swamp of relativism. There would be no grounds for debating the foundations of Freudian,

Kleinian, and Lacanian schools of psychoanalysis (and neither that of "wild" psychoanalysis), and one could project into the mind/brain whatever agencies, processes, and entities he or she likes.

I think that there is no unambiguous solution to the dilemma between essentialist and nominalist views. In order to manage the problem, we should, first, be explicit as to whether we think that a certain psychoanalytic concept is a construct, or refers to an enity (or process) existing in the mind or brain. Second, when holding that the concept in question refers to an existing entity or a process, we should show where and how it exists. If we think that a concept is a construct, we should argue why it is of use.

When thinking of psychoanalytic concepts in particular, the diversity of psychoanalytic theories and schools implies that it is extremely difficult to advocate the essentialist view. If our psychological reality consisted of distinctive psychological entities that psychological concepts pick up, how could psychoanalytic schools fail to recognise the relevance of other schools' concepts? Paul Stepansky holds that different psychoanalytic schools do not share clinical facts, since observations are always theory-laden—"Clinical 'facts', as Roy Schafer pointed out more than a decade ago, are supremely plastic; they do not exist outside the particular narrative story line in which they are conceptualized and embedded" (Stepansky, 2009, p. 242). Christopher Bollas seems to think that the theory-ladeness of clinical facts holds on a personal level, too: "[I]ndeed, experienced analysts of the same school of thought listening to the same chain of ideas would disagree over its latent meaning, and the same clinician may hear things differently according to his changing frames of mind" (Bollas, 1995, p. 11).

The considerations of this chapter imply, first, that psychoanalytic concepts cannot help from being theory-laden constructs, and second, this state of things by no means challenges the scientific status of psychoanalysis. To put it another way, the variety of psychoanalytic theories and models is not a serious problem: it is legitimate to construct analysands' problems from several perspectives, and due to the nature of psychology, it is difficult to state the relations of those theories in an exact manner.

I am aware that many psychoanalytic thinkers do not agree with this conclusion (and that some other thinkers were very eager to accept it), and that is by no means a basic assumption of the rest of the book—actually, in what follows I will argue in favour of my view from several viewpoints. Regardless of whether one advocates a nominalist or an essentialistic view on psychoanalytic concepts, it is nevertheless clear that, as an endeavour, psychoanalysis should be self-conscious concerning the essence and interrelations of its many theories. Let us end this chapter with a scheme that can be used in various contexts in order to tighten up the meanings and points of reference of psychoanalytic terms.

A scheme for the study of the essence of psychoanalytic concepts

When aiming at promote mutual understanding between psychoanalytic schools, and psychoanalytic and non-psychoanalytic students, it is important to pinpoint and explicate disagreements. On the level of terminology this can be done by studying the terms of each one's background theories with the help of the scheme below.

Does the term in question refer to existing entities/processes or is it a construct?

If it refers to entities or processes:

- On what basis should we presume that it/they exist—what proves that the entity/process exists?
- If some professionals think that the concept is indeed a construct, what are their arguments?
- Why should those arguments be considered as bad?
- If there are psychoanalytic schools that do not accept the concept, what are their arguments?
- Why should those arguments be considered as bad?

If the term is a construct:

- Why should we use the term?
- If some professionals think that the concept actually refers to existing entities or processes, what are their arguments?
- Why should those arguments be considered as being bad?
- What are the concepts closest to this one, and what crucial difference does this one make?
- Is the concept dependent on a certain psychoanalytic or non-psychoanalytic model?
- Why is it reasonable to commit to that model?
- If there are psychoanalytic schools that do not accept the concept, what are their arguments?
- Why should those arguments be considered as bad?

CHAPTER TWO

Psychoanalysis and its concepts II: the mereological fallacy and Freud's structural model

Due to Max Bennett and Peter Hacker's (2003) book *Philosophical Foundations of Neuroscience*, the mereological fallacy is currently a fresh topic in the domains of cognitive neuroscience and the philosophy of mind. "Mereology" is a philosophers' term, referring to a relation between a whole and its parts. Thus, when Bennett and Hacker (2003, pp. 68–107) talk about the "mereological fallacy", they are claiming that somewhere there is bad thinking concerning the relation between persons and their parts. Their target is neuroscientists, who talk about the brain—a part of the human being—as, for example, deciding and knowing matters. Below I aim at showing that behind the structural model (in which the id, ego, and super-ego play key roles) also hides the mereological fallacy.

On the foundational incompatibility of folk-psychology and present-day neuroscience

Philosophers of mind have disputed whether or not folk-psychology should be seen as theory. Basing on the considerations having been put forward in the previous chapter, we might say that it is *more* than a theory: it is the foundation on which we base our acts when interacting with others. Folk-psychology treats persons as deciding, desiring, fearing, and knowing matters, and implies a dualistic world view. Namely, the idea that we have free will is embedded in the parlance of folk-psychology, since it presupposes that we make decisions that are not determined by material matters. Folk-psychology presumes that we possess non-material mind that operates beyond the laws of nature.

It is not possible to resign oneself from folk-psychology neither in personal nor formal interactions: in courts, psychotherapist consultation rooms, and restaurants, among other locales, it is used to think that the others around possess desires and beliefs and make decisions. When someone steals your car or your spouse is unfaithful, it is difficult to approach the situation materistically, to withold from projecting free will and responsibility to the other ("He/she should not have done that!"). Hacker (2010) claims that when a child learns to use (folk-) psychological concepts, two matters take place. First, saying "It hurts" instead of crying, and saying "I want/know/fear that ... ", a child learns a wholly new form of behaviour. Second, a child also learns to "describe other people and to describe and explain their behaviour in these [folk-psychological] terms" (pp. 5–6). Thus, when mastering the use of folk-psychological concepts, a child steps into a new world.

Dualism is, of course, intolerable from the perspectives of neuroscience, the philosophy of science, and the philosophy of mind. The most unconditional materialists (eliminative materialists) deny that we have a mind that folk-psychology presumes. Liberal materialists (emergent materialists, monists) concede the existence of mental phenomena, but hold that they are—somehow—basically material. Even if a materialist accepts the existence of mental phenomena, he or she cannot—as Kim (2005) has convincingly shown—accept the idea that mental matters would have causal power. Thus, for a materialist, a content of consciousness (for example, a desire) cannot make one cry or go to a bar, since it is only the material brain that is able to cause such things. One state of consciousness (thinking of, for example, poor people in developing countries) can neither cause another (feeling guilty), since according to Kim's line of thinking the causality has to be stated via the brain.

A lay person, a psychotherapist, a psychiatrist, and a clinical psychologist (and even less a judge) cannot, of course, accept this materialist view. As a matter of fact, for those professionals it appears as a ridiculous doctrine that denies the true essence of the human being. As Bem and Looren de Jong put it:

> If cogitation and desiring do not make a real causal difference, then agency, responsibility, crime and punishment have to be given up, and the foundations of society are shaken. We need mental causation as part of our view of persons, society and law, since we can blame only intentional persons, whose thoughts have effects in the world—not machines, or brains.
>
> (Bem and Looren de Jong, 2006, p. 250)

No clinician can base on materialism, since if pains and suffering were not extremely real and important aspects of human life, relieving them would not be worth the huge diligence of clinicians and researchers.

Dualistic ideas have been for decades almost taboo in the scope of the philosophy of mind, and by challenging the materialistic foundations of science a philosopher might thus jeopardise his or her professional reputation. In recent years, however, there has emerged some notable criticism towards materialistic doctrines which take seriously our lay-person intuitions (Koons & Bealer, 2010; Pockett, Banks & Callagher, 2006).

Bennett and Hacker open the chapter treating the mereological fallacy (Bennett & Hacker, 2003, pp. 68–107) by stating that whilst the two first generations of neuroscientists were Cartesians (dualists), the third generation repudiated dualism, but began to ascribe mental characteristics to the (parts of the) brain. In Bennett and Hacker's reading, the mereological fallacy—which we study below in detail—camouflages present-day neuroscientists' materialism, which otherwise would seem non-realistic to people.

There are many ways to hide or downplay the mind–body problem, and talk about "levels" is strictly speaking among them. In the behavioural sciences talk about different levels of explanation is very common. In the philosophy of psychology it is talked about "personal level" and "sub-personal level" explanations. The former refers to the vocabulary of folk-psychology (deciding, knowing, and so forth), whereas the latter, the "sub-personal level", is concerned with neural or mental mechanisms that are not accessible to introspection. In present-day discussions, sub-personal explanations are those presented by neuroscientists. The term "level" implies that there are hierarchical viewpoints, which are not contradictory—similar to, for example, how photosynthesis may be explained in a non-contradictory manner at the levels of both atoms and molecules.

It is difficult to avoid talking about levels of explanation in the behavioural sciences, and the reader will note that I do not succeed in avoiding that habit of talk either. Anyway, it has to be conceded that the talk about personal and sub-personal *levels* of explanation is misleading: that way of talking *blurs the foundational contradiction between folk-psychology (personal level study) and neuroscience (sub-personal level).* The former is openly dualistic, the latter materialistic. It is more appropriate to talk about different kinds of explanation. Since the relations between psychology and neuroscience will be studied in a profound manner in the following two chapters, we can now turn to Bennett and Hacker's claims.

Psychologicising the brain—Bennett and Hacker on the mereological fallacy in neuroscience

Max Bennett and Peter Hacker (2003, pp. 68–70) illustrate the habit of talk that realises the mereological fallacy by citing well-known neuroscientists: Francis Crick states that the brain makes *interpretations, believes* certain matters, *combines information,* and *makes guesses;* Gerald Edelman is cited to hold that certain structures of the brain *categorise, discriminate,* and *recombine* things, and that "the brain relates semantic to phonological sequences and then generates syntactic correspondences"; Colin Blakemore claims that certain neurons have *knowledge* and *intelligence,* and that they "present arguments to the brain"; Antonio Damasio and Benjamin Libet are cited stating that brains can *decide;* and David Marr is claimed to hold that the brain represents information and makes it available.

The moral is that such a habit of talk is very common among the leading neuroscientists, and Bennett and Hacker ask whether we deal here with discovery, linguistic innovation, or plain confusion. They answer by stating that it is nonsense to claim that the brain or parts of it would possess the things or do the activities mentioned above. Below I present the logic of the mereological fallacy in a—I hope—more accessible manner than Bennett and Hacker (2003, pp. 68–71).

As presented in the first chapter, behind the folk-psychological terms like "believe" and "desire" there lean some background presuppositions.

People are supposed to possess phenomenal consciousness, and in the stream of consciousness it is thought to appear ideas, which are related to one another through thought processess. When a person is said to, for example, *decide* something, it means that he or she considers the alternatives of the decision in their consciousness—one may contemplate options A, B, and C, and decide by some criteria on A. Similarly, phrases like "to interpret", "to desire", and "to know" imply certain kinds of matters taking place in one's phenomenal consciousness. To put it in other words, (at least part of) the concepts of folk-psychology imply that people possess free will—it would not make sense to say that a person decides A, if he or she had not had also the possibility to decide at least B.

No one thinks that that the brain or its parts (a neuron, a neural network) possesses phenomenal consciousness or free will. If we take phenomenal consciousness and free will away from deciding, what does the term mean? Surely something different, and perhaps nothing. Thus, it seems that Bennett and Hacker are on the right track when criticising neuroscience from the point of view of the mereological fallacy.

Flowers may be said to "decide" to turn towards the Sun, thermostats to "turn off" the heater, and computers to "recognise" a virus. We might also say that plants, thermostats, and computers possess knowledge, are intelligent (because of being able to do such reasonable matters), and interpret their environment. Actually, such a habit of talk is rather common in our everyday life.

When using psychological terms this way, we are playing, or talking metaphorically—we know that plants, thermostats, and computers do not actually decide or know anything. Instead, their composition determines their reactions in every detail. Their behaviour may be flexible, but behind it there is no comprehension of alternatives. All in all, plants, thermostats, and computers *function in a fully mechanistic manner*. Neurons, neural networks, and the brain also function that way: neurobiological matters, electro-chemical impulses in the first hand, determine the functioning of them altogether.

Before the third-generation neuroscientists began to psychologise the brain, neurophysical processes had already been used to make descriptions on an abstract level. First, there has been talk about neural networks being able to *detect* stimuli. This means that when certain pattern of stimuli (for example, a certain habit of speech or certain visual form) is perceived through the senses, certain neural networks become active. It has been found that this may happen even without conscious processing. "Detect" is a wholly correct neuroscientific term, since it reflects the actual (mechanical) functioning of the brain, and does not contain similar implications as psychological terms. Second, the detection of a (pattern of) stimuli has often been found to lead to a *triggering of neural algorithms*. When, for example, a stimulus which has appeared previously in a dangerous situation is detected, detection may trigger fight-or-flight reactions. The triggering of the neural algorithms does not imply free will or any kind of mental matter. Joseph Le Doux's (1998) and Gerald Edelman's (Edelman & Tononi, 2000) studies, among others, illustrate how we can understand the neurophysiological basis of our behaviour through the terms "detection" and "neural algorithms".

The concepts of folk-psychology are not detached words, but rather form a system, where the parts are tied to one another. Bennet and Hacker remind us that extending the meaning of psychological terms (or using the terms in a metaphorical sense) makes the system collapse. For instance, knowledge of personally important matters (the serious illness of a close friend, or the dangerousness of an incoming situation, for example) affects one's feelings, creating ambivalence as one has to choose between alternatives and possibly causing anxiety or feelings of guilt as one has to make decisions. "Knowledge" and "choices" of the brain lack such interactive characteristics. Both lay-person knowledge and empirical research also inform us that mental processes are affected by, for example, tiredness, troubles, and hormonal matters. Neural structures and processes lack this kind of dynamics: it would be absurd to state that due to tiredness, a neural structure chooses today different things than previously.

All in all it seems clear that Bennett and Hacker have an obscure phenomenon under their thumbs. We must ask what the third-generation neuroscientists have in mind when ascribing psychological attributes to the brain, which functions in a wholly mechanistical manner. My guess is that neuroscientists, fascinated with new discoveries, made possible by new equipment, want to popularise their findings, making them understandable for the general audience. Bennett and Hacker's notion (or claim) that psychologisation of the brain goes hand in hand with the abandonment of Cartesian dualism also gives rise to a conspirative interpretation: perhaps the function of the habit of talk is to camouflage the materialistic worldview.

Anyway, Bennett and Hacker introduce three possible rationales behind the neuroscientists' habit of talk. First, it might be thought that neuroscientists use psychological terms in a technical sense, and thus they are actually *homonyms*—when saying that the brain "believes" or "decides" something, the meaning is different from our everyday talk about persons believing or deciding. However, Bennett and Hacker state that when reading neuroscientists' texts, it becomes evident that those terms are not used in a technical sense. Second, neuroscientists may *extend the ordinary use of psychological vocabulary*. Third, their talk may be *metaphorical* or *figurative*. Bennett and Hacker seem to possess good reasons for talking about the (mereological) *fallacy* in particular: whichever of the above alternatives is right, the rationale behind psychologising the brain is very confused.

The structural model and the mereological fallacy—are the id, the ego, and the super-ego supposed to be persons?

Perhaps the reader already detected the similarity between the third-generation neuroscientists' way of talking about the brain and certain psychoanalytic habits of talk. Namely, in his structural model, Freud *antropomorphised* the mind, that is, he treated the agencies of the mind as if they were persons. In order to illustrate this, let us pick from "The ego and the id" (Freud, 1923b) some of Freud's expressions.

First, it has to be noted that Freud sees the ego's task as rather demanding:

> As a frontier-creature, the ego tries to mediate between the world and the id, to make the id pliable to the world and, by means of its muscular activity, to make the world fall in with the wishes of the id.
>
> (Freud, 1923b, p. 56)

The ego is also able to notice the existence of the analyst, and tries to affect him or her:

> Consequently the patient's ego rebels against the imputation of guilt and seeks the physician's support in repudiating it.
>
> (Freud, 1923b, p. 51)

In order to cope with its demanding tasks, the ego has to be supposed to possess humanlike cognitive competencies. Thus it is perhaps not a surprise that Freud presumes the ego to possess also self-consciousness:

> [I]t [the Ego] is the mental agency which supervises all its own constituent processes.
>
> (Freud, 1923b, p. 17).

Similar to humans, it also has a sleep pattern:

> [[T]he ego] goes to sleep at night, though even then it exercises the censorship on dreams.
>
> (Freud, 1923b, p. 17)

According to Freud, the ego has experiences, phenomenal consciousness:

> What it is that the ego fears from the external and from the libidinal danger cannot be specified.
>
> (Freud, 1923b, p. 57)

This is also the case with the id:

> [E]go can obtain control over the id and deepen its relations with it—at the cost, it is true, of acquiescing to a large extent in the id's experiences.
>
> (Freud, 1923b, p. 30)

The id is also a store of episodic memory:

> With the aid of the super-ego, in a manner that is still obscure to us, it draws upon the experiences of past ages stored in the id.
>
> (Freud, 1923b, p. 55)

The super-ego may be the shallowest of the three agents. However, there is no doubt that it, too, possesses notable cognitive competencies:

> The super-ego, however, behaves as if the ego were responsible for them and shows at the same time by the seriousness with which it chastises these destructive intentions that they are no mere semblance evoked by regression but an actual substitution of hate for love.
>
> (Freud, 1923b, p. 53)

Similar to humans, the agencies have passionate interrelations:

> When the ego assumes the features of the object, it is forcing itself, so to speak, upon the id as a love-object and is trying to make good the id's loss by saying: "Look, you can love me too—I am so like the object."
>
> (Freud, 1923b, p. 30)

> The fear of death in melancholia only admits of one explanation: that the ego gives itself up because it feels itself hated and persecuted by the super-ego, instead of loved. To the ego, therefore, living means the same as being loved—being loved by the super-ego, which here again appears as the representative of the id.
>
> (Freud, 1923b, p. 58)

> How is it that the super-ego ... develops such extraordinary harshness and severity towards the ego? ... strong super-ego which has obtained a hold upon consciousness rages against the ego with merciless violence, as if it had taken possession of the whole of the sadism available in the person concerned ... and in fact it often enough succeeds in driving the ego into death, if the latter does not fend off its tyrant in time by the change round into mania.
>
> (Freud, 1923b, p. 53)

> Helpless in both directions, the ego defends itself vainly, alike against the instigations of the murderous id and against the reproaches of the punishing conscience.
>
> (Freud, 1923b, p. 53)

Between the agencies there seems to be a family-drama meeting the highest Shakespearian standards.

Freud also presents metaphors of the characteristics and interrelations of the agencies. In this he follows Plato:

> Thus in its relation to the id it is like a man on horseback, who has to hold in check the superior strength of the horse; with this difference, that the rider tries to do so with his own strength while the ego uses borrowed forces. The analogy may be carried a little further. Often a rider, if he is not to be parted from his horse, is obliged to guide it where it wants to go.
>
> (Freud, 1923b, p. 25)

Let us take another metaphor:

> [I]n the matter of action the ego's position is like that of a constitutional monarch, without whose sanction no law can be passed but who hesitates long before imposing his veto on any measure put forward by Parliament.
>
> (Freud, 1923b, p. 55)

All in all it is appropriate to state that Freud descibes the ego, the id, and the super-ego as humanlike agencies, persons, who are intelligent and possess phenomenal consciousness. As Bennet and Hacker (2003, p. 71) remind us, the homunculus fallacy is one perspective to the mereological fallacy. Let us study the structural model in terms of it.

The homunculus fallacy and the structural model

In the psychological literature the term "homunculus" pops up in several contexts. "Homunculus" means "a miniature", "a little man". Neuroscientists talk about "cortical homunculus", which is a pictorial representation of how parts of the cortex are responsible for motor and sensory information about different parts of the body. Cortical homunculus may be an oversimplification, but the basic idea is not especially fallacious.

The phrase "homunculus fallacy", for its part, refers to a certain kind of erroneous, often implicit, explanatory strategy. Psychology aims at explaining people's different kind of mental and behavioural competencies, defects, and other phenomena—the ability to treat sense-data in order to form representations of the outer world; competencies and skills like riding a bicycle; psychic disorders; and so on. The task of psychology is to explain people's reactions, and the presupposition of homunculus leads to an infinite regression: it in a certain way "explains" the phenomenon, but then we should explain how the wise homunculus, strongly resembling people, is able to do its task. The answer is that inside it there is another homunculus ... (see, for example, Dennett, 1991).

Let us think of our visual system. The outer world becomes reflected on the retina of the eye, and the receptors of the retina are connected to the neurons of the visual cortex. Different regions of the cortex, distinct neural networks, or information-processing modules, are spesialised in the different aspects of perception: colours, certain kinds of shapes (circles, lines, etc.), and certain kinds of movement (from left to right, from right to left, etc.). The modules function independently, and, for example, neural networks processing colours do not interact with those processing forms. Astonishingly, the activity of distinct modules nevertheless leads to a unified visual experience—one sees a goalkeeper wearing a red shirt catching the ball by jumping to the left, for instance. That is, in one's experience red is correctly located in the goalkeeper's shirt, and the goalkeeper is seen as moving as a unified character. This leads to the question of how the mechanistic functioning of simple independent modules leads to a unified visual experience. This question is difficult to answer, and researchers talk about "the binding problem" (see, for example, Robertson, 2003).

There is a temptation to think that someone is looking at the picture becoming reflected on the retina, or that the outcomes of the processing of the modules are being directed into the monitor room, where someone would edit the unified visual experience from raw data. These ideas represent explicitly the homunculus fallacy, since nobody is watching the retina, and there are no little men in our brains.

Usually a neurophysiological theory falls implicitly to the fallacy by suggesting that a certain region of the brain is responsible for the experience or competence by choosing, interpreting, or editing information, or making decisions. However, only humans are able to do such things.

Let us note that it is fallacious to presume a "wise" homunculus, but as Marvin Minsky infamously claimed in his book *The Society of*

Mind (Minsky, 1988), it is legitimate to presume an army of "dumb" homunculi. As a matter of fact, the latter explanatory strategy is prevalent in the domain of cognitive neuroscience. The brain has been found to contain a huge amount of specialised information-processing modules, which are dumb; that is, they act mechanically in a certain restricted field. This means that they just detect stimuli in their field, and trigger neural algorithms.

When studying the above citations from "The ego and the id" from this viewpoint, it is difficult to escape from thinking that in the core of Freud's structural model we find the homunculus fallacy: Freud explains psychic disorders by presupposing (at least) three wise homunculi in our heads.

The homunculus-problem of Freud's thinking is something commonly recognised (for example, Haldane, 1988). In order to illustrate the issue from an unconventional and non-technical perspective, let us ask how do we know which psychological attributes may or may not be used when talking about those Freudian agencies of the mind? If the id, the ego, and the super-ego are such humanlike creatures, should not we treat them like humans ought to be treated (and avoid, for example, hurting them)? Could we explain a person's behaviour by claiming that his ego was tired or exhausted, or that his id was hyperactive, or that the super-ego did not bother to concentrate to its task(s)?

The former question concerning the human rights of the agencies is rather provocative and difficult to grasp. However, it is worth thinking how could we know that it is plausible to antropomorphise the mind like Freud did, but that we should not talk about, for example, tiredness or hyperactivity of the agencies. Consider someone creating an alternative structural theory, according to which certain disorders are due to the hyperactivity of the id or exhaustion of the ego. Our rebellious analyst might argue that if the ego may feel itself hated or loved, who says that it could not feel tired?

Nobody has ever made observations on the id, the ego, and the super-ego, and thus both the Freudian and the outlaw structural models are based on certain interpretations of people's behaviour. I think it would not be possible to reach a consensus on the charateristics of the agencies on this basis—the only argument against the outlaw model was that *the ego and the id do not possess such characteristics because Freud did not think that way.*

In addition to the characteristics of the agents, we should also consider the number of them. Sharpe (1988, p. 194) asks why should we stop at three—why not specify an agent for each desire? All in all, talk about the agencies of the mind is always somewhat arbitrary: since there are actually no people in our minds, there is no method to detemine the rules for antropomorphising the mind.

I think it is appropriate to state that in his structural model Freud did something very similar to the third-generation neuroscientists when ascribing or projecting characteristics to the parts of man. There is one vocabulary for whole persons presuming phenomenal consciousness and free will ("feeling", "deciding", "interpreting"...), and another for people's parts representing the mechanical functioning of a (neural) system ("causing", "activating", "detecting", "triggering"...). Freud mixes these vocabularies, and thus it is not clear how the structural model should be seen in the frames of science and scientific explanations.

Mental apparatus as construct

As mentioned, Bennett and Hacker treat three objections against their critique: neuroscientists use psychological terms in a technical sense; extend the ordinary use of psychological vocabulary; or talk metaphorically. Could the psychoanalytic way of talking about the furniture of the mind/brain be justified on this basis?

Part of psychoanalytic concepts are surely technical terms. Unconscious desires, beliefs, and fears, however, are not among them. Freud leaned on our everyday meaning of those words and argued that desires, and so forth, may also be unconscious.

Not surprisingly, it is commonly claimed that Freud extended the use of folk-psychological terms into the domain of the unconscious. Whether or not such an extension is plausible, that seems to be a correct characterisation of his thinking (or at least part of it). Anyway, claiming that the structural model is an extension of folk-pyschology does not make the agents of the mind real.

When it comes to metaphors, many advocates of psychoanalysis would state that *of course* Freud's structural model should be taken metaphorically: it would make no sense to think that, for example, while reading this text, those instances were lying down (or standing, or running) in your head monitoring you, me (through the text), and one another. In this state of affairs it is important to go beyond the metaphors, and be explicit on what psychoanalytic terms are supposed to refer to.

It is possible and, I think, reasonable, to hold that the id, the ego, and the super-ego (and actually the whole mental apparatus, see Talvitie & Ihanus, 2006) are constructs. Sometimes impulses—aggressive and sexual, at least—take place in us; that is, we face a strong pressure or temptation to act in a certain way (the id). It is also clear that we have different—better or worse, more or less flexible—capacities to live with the impulses (the ego). Nobody denies that also values, ideals, rules, and principles entertain a crucial role in human life (the super-ego). We might say that the structural model comprehends the aspects of human life crucial from the psychotherapeutic viewpoint, and there is no reason to doubt that the model may help a psychodynamic therapist to approach the dynamics of their client's mental life.

These aspects of our mental life surely possess neural correlates, and thus Freud (1923b, p. 26) stated: "If we wish to find an anatomical analogy for it [the ego] we can best identify it with the 'cortical homunculus' of the anatomists, which stands on its head in the cortex, sticks up its heels, faces backwards and, as we know, has its speech-area on the left-hand side." However, the agencies cover a variety of complex and dynamic phenomena, and it is hopeless to determine their exact neural correlates.

When explicating the metaphorical talk about the agencies and describing their existence in a manner that is reasonable in terms of cognitive neuroscience, they appear—similar to the neural structures behind vision, for example—as bunches of modules, neural networks, or "dumb" homunculi, working in an integrated manner. As far as the agencies presumed by Freud's structural model are thought to exist (behind metaphorical talk) in only this way, there is no problem with academic research.

Concluding remarks

Before focusing in the next chapter on the nature of psychological and psychoanalytic explanations, let us make some general notions on the essence of psychological concepts. Basing on the consideration of the first two chapters, we are able to see three crucial differences between the natural sciences and psychology. First, psychology is strongly dependent on the terms—we might also say *worldview*—of folk-psychology. Folk-psychology is a powerful, but nevertheless, non-scientific, view. The natural sciences lack this kind of connection to lay-person views.

Second, behind psychology always lurks the mind–body problem, which causes at least inconsistency to the explanations presented by different branches of the behavioural sciences. According to common sense, mental matters (for example, feelings and desires) possess causal power, that is, they affect both other mental matters, and how we behave. In the scope of strict materialistic science it is questionable as to whether mental matters may exist (without violating the materialistic conception), and at least they cannot possess causal power. Thus, if there are psychological explanations that are satisfying in a strict materialistic sense, they cannot be mentalistic. This state of things appears, of course, as absurd for all clinicians and their clients.

Third, psychological concepts are for the most part constructs, whereas natural scientists' concepts can—generally speaking—be tied more intimately to the measurements and observations having been made with different kinds of equipment. Thus, natural scientists may reach a consensus on the existence of atoms, planets, viruses, and deoxyribonucleic acid (DNA), and the essentialist position is easier to defend. Closely related to this, the natural sciences are also able to present causal relations and laws of nature. Let us, however, mention that a rather radical branch of the sociology of science originating from Latour and Woolgar's (1979) classic study maintains that scientists, too, construct facts in their laboratories.

Thus, psychological concepts are far from the world of the natural sciences. We can be sure of the existence of just experiences occuring in the scope of consciousness and the neurophysiological structures of the brain. Everything that may lie between them can be claimed to be constructs. In those constructs, three distinct spheres become amalgamated: experiences; patterns of behaviour and reactions (behavioural dispositions); and habits of talk of the surrounding culture (folk-psychology) that have emerged in order to serve social interaction. Due to this three-fold nature of psychological concepts, in the world of psychology the interrelations between different concepts, measurements, observations, and theories cannot be determined in such precision as is the case in the domain of the natural sciences.

CHAPTER THREE

What are psychological and psychoanalytic explanations like? (And how that should change the way we see psychoanalytic theories)

In the last two chapters we focused on parts (psychological concepts), and below we turn sight to the wholes that are built from them—theories and explanations. I will focus on three topics. First, the relation between psychological and neurobiological explanations; second, the nature of causes in general, and the causes of psychic disorders in particular, which shall be closely related to a critique presented by Adolf Grünbaum; and third, the consequences of the fact that psychoanalysis is interested in idiosynchratic phenomena. At the end of the chapter I will study the notable implications these considerations bear on what we should think about the nature of psychoanalytic theories. We will begin, however, with the study on whether it is possible to reveal laws in the domains of psychoanalysis and other psychological disciplines.

Are there laws in the domain of psychology?

Could we claim that when considering, for example, all people whose Oedipal conflict is unresolved, they all have had certain particular problems with early development, or that each of their ability for mentalisation is restricted in a certain particular manner? Or when having certain repressed intrapsychic conflicts, the consequence is *always* a certain psychic disorder or characteristic of personality? Even if just one of these such claims were justifiable, it would mean that psychology can, similar to the natural sciences, present laws.

When claiming that A causes B, in science there are two basic routes to justify the claim. For the first, a scientist may argue (in the spirit originating from C. G. Hempel's covering law model) that the causal connection is due to a law of nature. For the second, he or she may try to show through statistical methods (in the "Bayesian spirit") that B follows A (see, for example, Rosenberg, 2000).

Since Robert Cummins' *The Nature of Psychological Explanation* (Cummins, 1983) it has been thought that psychology cannot present (universal) causal laws (see, for example, Kim, 2010, pp. 282–319). Thus, also Stanovitch states: "Virtually all the facts and relationships that have been uncovered by the science of psychology are stated in terms of probabilities" (Stanovitch, 2000, p. 155). In order to illustrate the difficulty of pinpointing psychological laws, let us think of the probably most general and widely accepted statement in the domain of psychology—"Miller's law" concerning the "magical number seven". That "law" in question refers to George A. Miller's suggestion from the year 1956 that the capacity of the working-memory is 7+/–2 chunks. Note that although we deal here with foundational cognitive characteristics shared by the whole of humankind, researchers end up with a very vague description ("+/–2"). Actually, Miller (1956) used the expression "magical number seven" in an ironic sense. All in all, from the viewpoint of natural science, talk about *law* is here a remarkable overstatement.

Let us consider how do the most ordinary psychological phenomena appear from the perspective of laws ("When A, always B"). When something sad happens, does a human always become sad? No. When a human faces an insult, does he or she always feel hurt? No. When a neural tissue in, say, a finger, becomes damaged in ordinary conditions (when one is not, for example, under anaesthetic), does a human always feel pain? No. There seems to be no reason to doubt Cummins' claim that psychology is not a discipline of laws. Actually, according to the commonly accepted view (for example, Fodor, 1989; Kim, 2010, pp. 282–319) we cannot find laws from the domains of other special sciences either.

Jaegwon Kim thinks that there are no *biological* laws since "nonbiological physical events (exposure to high levels of radiation, the unavailability of necessary nutrients, ecological changes, natural disasters, and so on) can always intervene to break up biological causal processes" (Kim, 2010, p. 292). We might say that foundational physical processes are "stronger" than those studied by special sciences. According to Kim the multi-realisation of mental properties, studied more thoroughly in the next chapter, is another reason why there are no laws in the domain of psychology. To put it shortly, he holds that since all people are unique (similarly as "say, all samples of the 2006 Honda Accord LX Sedan" (Kim 2010, 301)), we cannot find laws without exceptions.

Thus, should psychoanalysis also avoid sketching universal laws, and restrict itself to probabilities—no universal Oedipus complex, no universal claims about developmental matters (in terms of, for example, stages of psychosexual development and Kleinian positions), no general principles of mental functioning, no wish-fulfilment behind every dream? In any case, it is extremely unlikely that psychoanalysis could reveal an exceptionless law in the domain of psychology. Revealing such a law was a sensation in the philosophy of science. Although many psychoanalytic thinkers would miss those strict Freudian principles, giving up the universal claims concerning the essence of humans is reasonable, since that made the burden of the proof of theories considerably lighter.

On psychological and neurobiological explanations

When considering the essence of psychology and psychological explanations, two big names from the history of psychology have to be mentioned. First, Freud's teacher, the philosopher Franz Brentano, who published *Psychologie vom empirischen Standpunkt* (*Psychology from an Empirical Standpoint*) in 1874. Second, the cognitive scientist Robert Cummins, mentioned above, who wrote the classic *The Nature of Psychological Explanation* (1983). In some circles the rapid development of neuroscience has given rise to the idea that neurobiological explanations will make psychological explanations redundant (which has surely something to do with the mereological fallacy studied in the previous chapter). Thus, the rise of neuroscience and biological psychiatry has made the question concerning the essence of psychology topical, and in the domains of both the philosophy of psychiatry and the philosophy of psychology there is a vast literature on it (for example, Bermúdez, 2005;

Kendler & Parnas, 2008; Schouten & Looren de Jong, 2007). Let us make here the notion that neuropsychoanalytic writings make little reference to this literature, which reflects the shallowness and non-reflective enthusiasm of the discipline.

One might think that psychology and neurobiology possess territories of their own, and as a consequence psychological phenomena were searched for and given psychological explanations, and neurobiological phenomena neurobiological explanations. The situation is not that simple, however. In some cases a neurobiological explanation is clearly the correct one for a psychological phenomenon—when one is given a certain kind of drug, he or she becomes hyperactive or calm, for example. Similarly, a psychological explanation is sometimes the one which we feel is the most plausible for a physiological phenomenon: perceiving or thinking of a frightening matter may accelerate heart beat, and psychological stress may affect levels of hormones.

When approaching the relation between psychological and neurobiological explanations it is important to be sensitive as to *how the phenomenon under scrutiny is described*. If the phenomenon aimed at being explained is "why Jane's hand rose", there is no room for psychological explanation, and the explanation is to be given in terms of neuroscience—that happened because of certain neural activity in Jane's body and brain. If we describe the same phenomenon by telling that Jane rose her hand in order to vote for Hank as president of the club, the situation is radically different: that description opens up a plethora of psychological issues.

When studying Jane's act on the foundational level of cognitions studied by cognitive science, we make the notion that Jane supposedly knows what is an election, what is a president, that the current social situation is an election, and so on. These issues fall in the domain of knowledge-representation treated in the first chapter.

Psychoanalytically interesting issues emerge if we ask why Jane voted for Hank instead of Waylon. Such a conceptualisation leads us to study why Jane is a member of the organisation in the scope of which the election takes place, what desires and fantasies she has about it, what desires and hopes does she possess towards Hank (and Waylon), and so on. From the psychological point of view it would be interesting if Jane had planned to vote for Waylon, and rose her hand by accident—what would be the explanation for that slip? The above considerations lead us to a view, commonly accepted in the domain of the philosophy of science (for example, Godfrey-Smith, 2003; van Fraassen, 2008; Wimsatt, 2007): the appropriateness of an explanation *depends on one's viewpoint and interests.*

Inside the realm of psychology there are a considerable number of differing viewpoints and interests. Psychotherapists, and in that way also the theories behind psychotherapy schools, focus on idiosyncratic phenomena—why does this particular person possess these disorders? Contrary to that, the interests of cognitive science, evolutionary psychology, and the neurosciences, lie on a species-specific level, bracketing individual differences. For example, evolutionary psychology can tell why women in general, or probabilistically, prefer certain kinds of men. Applying this kind of matter to individual cases is a complicated affair—how and to what extent this kind of evolutionary matter has a bearing on, for example, why Jane voted for Hank.

If Hank possesses features that women are attractived to, that (unconscious) factor only makes it more probable that Jane and other women shall vote for him. However, other matters may also overhelm the evolutionary factor. These considerations bring us to the preliminary conclusion that perhaps we should not search for a single (correct) explanation for phenomena. Instead, there are several psychological, social, and neurobiological matters that cause, or at least affect, how we feel, react, and behave.

Causes, reasons, and clinician's realism

Cause is a metaphysical concept. Non-philosophers tend to think that if B always follows A, some kind of power, force, or energy has to be responsible for that state of things. However, David Hume challenged that traditional conception and argued that causation is an empirical matter: we talk about causes only because we have noted that B always follows A. According to the Humean lines of thought, popular among present-day philosophers, a cause is a theoretical concept, and causal relation is something *we project into the world*. Let us note here that even in the domain of natural science it is very difficult to show a strict causal relationship. (Chalmers, 1999; Loux, 2006, pp. 187–204; Rosenberg, 2000, pp. 21–47)

It is often claimed that talk about causes belongs to the natural sciences, and the humanities focus on the *reasons* of behaviour. The logic behind the claim is that when it is searched for a cause for an occurrence in the physical world (for instance, the rising of a hand), a mentalistic explanation ("Jane rose her hand because she wanted to vote for Hank") does not specify the material cause of the occurrence (i.e., the activity of certain neural networks). When restricting the use of the term "cause" in the domain of natural science, one ensures that the materialistic doctrines do not become violated.

However, such a stand is against common sense; it is not *realistic*. Everybody "knows" that my desire to have a beer is the cause for going to the pub, and Jane's desire to vote for Hank was the cause for the lifting of her hand. Thus, it is sometimes argued that mental matters may also cause behaviour. Advocates of that view (for example, Bolton & Hill, 2003; Lennon, 1990) remind that mental states are coded in the brain, and thus materialistic doctrines do not become (seriously) violated by holding mental states as causes of behaviour. This issue is rather complicated (see Kim, 2005), but for our topic it is not necessary to go deeper into it—it is clear that clinicians cannot help from being "realists" here, and to think of desires, fears, memories, and fantasies as causing different matters.

Philosophers of science stress that behind different kinds of real-life occurrences and events we do not find a single cause. In the literature we often find the following example as illustrating this state of things: the causes of car accidents depend on if we focus on the driver(s), the car(s), the weather, or the road. Driver's error is not necessarily sufficient cause: if the brakes of the car had been better, or if the surface of the road had not been so slippery, the accident would not have happened.

Plurality of causes holds also with the current topic. Actually, when thinking of the relations between both neurobiology (or biological psychiatry) and psychology, and different schools of psychotherapy, it is extremely crucial to keep in mind that behind whatever disorder probably does not lie a single cause but actually several. Below I will shed light on this issue from several viewpoints. We will begin with the biologist Ernst Mayr's distinction between two kinds of causes.

Distal (ultimate) and proxal causes

Ernst Mayr talked about ultimate and proximate causes in order to characterise different branches of biology (for example, Mayr, 1997, pp. 107–123). When we think of, for instance, why giraffes have long necks, we find that genes are one cause. Another cause can be sketched through the evolutionary theory: giraffes with longer necks survived better than their shorter-necked fellow-creatures, and this is the cause for present-day giraffes' long necks. The former is a *proxal cause*, and the latter *distal* (or ultimate) one. It is evident that these two kinds of causes are not exclusive.

By applying Mayr's scheme we can make a chart on the different causes of psychic disorders. We can make, first, the distinction between psychological and neurobiological causes. The cause of depression, for example, may be stated in terms of intrapsychic conflicts (psychological causes), or by referring to the neurotransmitters of one's brain (neurobiological cause). Both causes may exist at the same time. Second, in the categories of both psychological and neurobiological causes there are distal and proxal causes. A distal psychological cause for depression may be found from early object-relations, and repression of certain desires may be a proxal psychological cause. A distal neurobiological cause may be, for example, a defect during the pre-natal period, and an imbalance of neurotransmitters a proxal neurobiological cause.

Distal and proxal causes are different sides of the same coin: the distal cause can be seen as setting the proxal cause in a historical context. Consider that the proxal cause of depression is repression of certain ideas. Represssion of that idea in particular, or use of repression as a defence in general, has historical origins, that is, distal cause. Usually the historical cause is not a particular event, a trauma, but rather a web of earlier experiences, or general conditions of early life. Similarly, the distal cause of a pre-natal defect has changed the brain, and a proxal cause of certain problems can be stated in terms of the neurophysiological consequences of the distal cause.

There are also connections between psychological and neurobiological causes. Presumably all mental matters possess neurophysical counterparts, and thus early psychic traumas have to be thought to change the brain. Thus, when the trauma later affects one's life, those psychic troubles possess both neurobiological and psychological distal causes. In such a case the psychological distal cause appears as the "orginal" cause, but in general it is not always clear whether psychological proceeds the neurobiological or vice versa.

Daniel Dennett (1987, pp. 13–35) has created a formal model of different kinds of explanation. Since I introduced his model already in *The Freudian Unconscious and Cognitive Neuroscience* (Talvitie, 2009, pp. 121–133), let us present here just a brief sketch of it. According to Dennett's model, there are three kinds of explanation. In order to stress that the appropriateness of an explanation is tied to a researcher's viewpoint and interests, Dennett talks about *stances*—one can approach phenomena in terms of physical stance, design stance, and intentional stance. "Physical stance" refers to the explanations of natural sciences, neurobiology among them. "Intentional stance" means that an organism's acts are made sense of in terms of its desires, beliefs, and fears (folk-psychology-type explanations). In the core of the middle level of explanation, "design stance", there are functions. When we tell that giraffes have long necks due to the logic of evolution (referring to the evolutionary function of a long neck), and that in a certain person garrulousness is a defence (a defensive function of verbosity), we present a design level explanation. Psychological explanations often mix intentional- and design level- perspectives.

The moral here is that it does not make sense to think that a disorder has either a neurobiological or psychological cause, or that it had just one cause. It is a difficult empirical issue as to what are the actual causes of a certain disorder. In principle, however, we must think that disorders may be approached from several perspectives, and there are several different causes behind them. The relevance of each of the causes depends on many matters. One cause may be something like a general boundary condition, which is interesting for an evolutionary psychologist, but not for a clinician.

A psychoanalytic reader may find the above lines of thought familiar. Namely, Freud stressed already in his early writings that dreams and disorders are multi-determined, and analytic candidates are sometimes taught to study their clients' problems from the topographical, structural, genetic (historical or developmental), energetic, and dynamic viewpoints. Familiarity may be also be due to the fact that the psychoanalytic tradition entails many different models and theories.

Causes of disorders—sketching the battleground around Adolf Grünbaum's critique

The issue of the causes of psychic disorders, and whether psychoanalysis has revealed these causes, has become under discussion through Adolf Grünbaum's works. Grünbaum has presented an influential critique concerning the scientific status of psychoanalysis, and his view has given rise to a very lively and extensive debate that has already lasted for almost three decades. The logic of his (for example, Grünbaum, 1993) main thesis may be stated as follows:

Freud presented psychoanalysis as an etiological theory, that states that repressed desires, traumatic experiences or sexual ideas are necessary and sufficient causes of disorders. However, it is not possible to verify causal claims basing on clinical material, i.e., case studies. Neo-Freudian psychoanalysis has suggested different etiologies for psychic disorders, but they share the basic problem of Freud's view: psychoanalysis presents causal explanations, but is not able to confirm them.

Psychoanalysts have reacted to Grünbaum's views in many ways, but rather often the logic of the defence is either that actually psychoanalysis *can* present causal explanations, or that psychoanalysis is a hermeneutic discipline that even *does* (or *should*) *not try* to do that. The above considerations on the plurality of causes hint that there is something wrong with the Freudo-Grünbaumian conception. Below we will see that when set in a wider context, the dispute around Grünbaum's critique appears as a battle, one which continues although the war—if such has ever been—is over.

The Grünbaum-battle is commonly known even outside the psychoanalytic circles, but it is rarely noticed that it does not necessarily have a lot to do with the psychoanalytic therapy as practised by present-day clinicians. Grünbaum and, for example, Edward Erwin (1996), restrict their studies to Freud's views, and I cannot avoid from thinking that they do so partly because Freud's hundred-year-old views are an easy target for criticism. Psychoanalysts and psychodynamic therapists that might advocate Freud's views as presented by Grünbaum and Erwin form a minority of the psychoanalytic community.

Since Freud's views are highly respected in psychoanalytic communities, analysts and therapists that are, say, "less Freudian", typically avoid presenting explicit criticism towards them. When talking about revisions of psychoanalytic theories, psychoanalytic folks often state in a somewhat obscure way that the revisions do not necessarily replace or contradict Freud's conceptions. Anyway, post-Freudian psychoanalysis has developed original conceptualisations on the causes of disorders and the aims of psychotherapy, and it is worth introducing briefly some of these.

Peter Fonagy, the former chairman of the International Psychoanalytic Association, and his collaborators, state: "The goal of therapy, then, is the observation of patterns of interaction and the identification and correction of maladative models, principally through strengthening an overarching mental capacity to activate alternative models of interaction selectively; in language influenced by cognitive science, this capacity may be labeled 'mentalization' or 'reflective function'" (Fonagy, Gergely, Jurist & Target, 2002, pp. 470–471). Thomas Ogden (1997, p. 15) believes "that the analytic task most fundamentally involves the effort of the analytic pair to help the analysand become human in a fuller sense than he has been able to achieve to this point. This is no abstract, philosophical quest; it is a requirement of the species as basic as the need for food and air." In his book treating the psychoanalytic treatment of people diagnosed as possessing a borderline personality organisation, Vamik Volkan states: "I focus on the therapeutic regression and subsequent progressive developments that occur over the course of lengthy and intense treatment in which the patient successfully identifies with some of the therapist's functions, particularly his ability to analyse and integrate" (Volkan, 1987, p. 1).

Some hermeneutic researchers like Jürgen Habermas and Paul Ricoeur hold—contrary to Freud—that psychoanalysis does not study causes but meanings (see, for example, Grünbaum, 1993, pp. 1–47). However, it is difficult to maintain both that a psychoanalytic cure often relieves the disorders and that the discussion between the therapist and a client has nothing to do with the causes of the disorders. As Erwin puts it, if the meanings "make a difference, if they do affect something, then they are causes. They may not enter into causal law; they may not be either causally necessary or causally sufficient, but they are causally relevant factors" (Erwin, 2010, p. 72; see also Grünbaum, 2004).

Erwin's view leads us to ask whether there is *a* cause behind Laura's depression or Larry's phobia, or if there are several causes. Grünbaum and Erwin base their critiques in a certain, perhaps somewhat inexact, reading of Freud: According to Freud, behind a psychic disorder there is always one, single cause. Moreover, behind the same kind of disorder (for example, paranoia) there lies always a similar cause.

Consider someone having seen a violent assault at the age of six, having had violent nightmares since that, and falling into psychosis after having seen a violent movie at the age of thirty. There seems to be evident relationships between early trauma, nightmares, and psychosis. Grünbaum (1993, pp. 109–166) calls this kind of relation "thematic kinships", and argues that thematic kinship does not justify the talk about causal relation. Erwin (2010, p. 73) agrees with him when considering a man promoting his attractive female supervisor, and his desire to have sex with her: it may be the case that the man's desire to have sex played no role (i.e., it is not a cause) in his promoting his supervisor.

Regardless if thematic kinship or meaning connection is *proof* for causal relationship, could there be, *in principle*, a causal relationship between the trauma on the one hand, and the nightmare and the psychosis on the other? Is it possible that an early trauma were a necessary and sufficient cause of the dreams and psychosis of later life?

If early trauma were a necessary and sufficient cause of the dreams and psychosis of later life, everyone having had experienced the trauma would have had nightmares, and suffered psychosis after having seen the violent movie. That is surely not true, and thus we cannot locate the cause in a single event. Generally speaking, it should be supposed that *behind disorders there are always several causes*: different (traumatic) experiences during the lifespan, genetic matters, and several properties of one's structure of mind or personality. This should not be news for any clinician.

When studying a psychoanalytic way to explain disorders and create theories, one should not treat psychoanalysis as an island, but rather take a look at the other disciplines that operate on the same field. The fields of psychiatry, psychology, and psychotherapy form the general context for the topic of the causes and explanations of psychic disorders. The multi-determination of disorders is widely accepted in psychiatry (see, for example, Bolton & Hill, 2003, pp. 241–278; Cooper, 2007, pp. 83–101; Mitchell, 2008; Murphy, 2008; Paris, 2008, pp. 6–9; Schaffner, 2008; Woodward, 2008). Let us cite John Cambell, who states: "My conclusion is that we should take at face value the flood of empirical work that suggests causation in psychiatry is multifactoral and the causal explanation will characteristically be 'many sorted', using variables of many different types" (Cambell, 2008, p. 214).

Considering the above mentioned mainstream view of psychiatry, we might say that it is a form of scientific mutilation to lean on a view that psychoanalysis could reveal *the* cause behind psychic disorders. A critic demanding that psychoanalysis presents the causes of a disorder appears undue, and a psychoanalyst presenting such causes appears as a megalomaniac. When the question concerning the scientific status of psychoanalysis is raised, psychoanalysis should be set not just in the context of psychiatry, but also that of the psychotherapies—are the psychotherapies scientific?

In addition to psychoanalysis, the only school of psychotherapy that at least tries to relate its methods and theories to the views of present-day research is cognitive psychotherapy. Similar to psychoanalysis, cognitive psychotherapy, too, has divided into several branches (cognitive-behavioural psychtherapy, cognitive-constructive psychotherapy, cognitive-analytic psychotherapy), and there is no shared view on the causes of disorders. All in all, we should not think as if there were some kind of battle between psychoanalytic folks and some Grünbaumians. Instead, we should ask whether such a practical and idiosyncratic affair as psychotherapy between two persons can be studied by the methods of science and humanities. Below we will approach this issue.

Idiosyncratic study and the networks of causes

Let me introduce still one more framework that enables us to make sense of the existence of several causes, and the logic between statistical and idiographic study. Mackie (1965, pp. 306–308) introduces the concept of "causal field", and when "influenza" of his original example is replaced with "depression", his idea appears as follows.

On the most general level, the question "What causes depression?" can be understood as calling for an answer of why some people "get" depression and some others do not. In that case the causal field is *human beings in general*. When recalling that certain matters (genetic liability and a certain kind of personal history) increase the probability of depression, we can see another, more restricted, causal field: *human beings possessing predispositions for depression*. In the scope of this field the question is why only a few people possessing those predispositions get depression. The "What causes depression?" question may be raised also in a singular case, and in that context the causal field may be seen in terms of the *career of the person* in question—why he or she developed depression at a particular age, and not sooner or later. Mackie reminds that "what is the cause in relation to one field may not be the cause in relation to another" (Mackie, 1965, p. 307).

The term "causal field" enables us to formalise the erroneousness of the Grünbaumian battlefield. Grünbaum's presupposition is the claim that according to Freud it is enough to think in terms of only one causal field—behind all depressions, hysterias, perversions, and so forth, there is a certain single cause. Regardless of whether or not Freud actually thought that way, in the current state of things the presupposition is foolish.

The network of the causes of disorders and the curative aspects of psychotherapy—or rather, how we conceptualise these two issues—intertwine in a complex manner. Psychic disorders may have such distal causes as pre-natal trauma, the death of a parent, and problems with early interaction with primary caretakers. An empirical study may show on a statistical level that such matters cause psychic disorders. When practising and studying psychotherapy, those kinds of causes are rather insignificant, since they describe only outer conditions, not a person's mind/brain. They are also very rough in their outline: the death of a parent, for example, is and may be traumatic in many different ways.

Outer conditions may be partial causes of disorders by affecting a person's mind/brain, or the functioning of it. In terms of Mayr's conceptualisation, these matters are distal causes, and conceptualising the distal causes of psychic disorders is a rather straightforward issue. The situation is radically different with proxal causes, since conceptualisation is always more theory-laden. We might present countless suggestions as to what kind of matters the early loss of a parent might give rise to. Or, to put it in other words, distal cause is basically just an event (death of a parent), characteristic of one's environment (nature of interaction with parents), or physical matter (pre-natal trauma), but there are numerous ways to conceptualise what kind of proxal cause it becomes transformed into.

For example, the following matters may be claimed as a proxal cause of a psychic disorder or other mental trouble: low self-esteem; proclivity to negative thinking; weak ego; fear of losing a close person (again); a strict super-ego; repressed desire; proclivity to feelings of guilt; and a low level of serotonin. As we see, many matters often suggested as a proxal cause are not "things in the head" but behavioural dispositions or other kinds of constructs (see the first chapter). It is easy to agree with Erwin stating:

> For a science of psychotherapy to exist, however, there need not be such [natural] laws [as in physics and chemistry]. It is enough that there be clinically significant true generalizations between certain

> causally relevant factors and certain effects ... they may be of the sort "under certain initial conditions, C, A-type events generally make an important causal difference to the occurrence of B-type events".
>
> (Erwin, 1997, p. 78)

After having approached so far the causes of disorders on a general level, or in principle, let us study therapists' knowledge concerning the networks of causes in a particular case after a long, successful therapy. Consider case studies, presented frequently in clinicians' congresses and journals. In some cases clinical data speaks in a convincing manner in favour of certain causes, and in some other cases disagreements emerge among clinicians. Disagreements tend to relate to the therapists' different theoretical backgrounds.

Let us still assume that a psychotherapist's client had been in comprehensive psychological test at the ages of, say, seven, fifteen, and thirty, and the psychologists' reports were available for clinicians. I think that the additional data would not change the basic picture: in some cases a consensus will emerge; in other cases clinicians disagree. (Erwin (1996, pp. 87–142) has presented a comprehensive study on the problems determining the causes of disorders basing on clinical case-study.) Actually this is the core problem of induction: when there is a claim X (for example, "all swans are white", or "Ben's disorders are caused by the gene X and his relationship to his mother"), it is not possible to determine what is the evidence that should be accepted as sufficient proof to validate the claim.

When we import this situation from the clinical context to the academic one, the crucial issue is that when studying the causes behind, for example, fermentation and photosynthesis, on the one hand, and the causes behind individuals' disorders and societies' revolutions on the other, we are in radically different fields of study. With the phenomena falling in the former category we can make experiments, but with the phenomena which would find their place in the latter it is very difficult to research the causes for several reasons. Consequently, talk about the causes of phenomena is on a much firmer ground with the phenomena of the former category. It is important to bear in mind that psychoanalysis is far from the only domain of research being not able to present the causes of the phenomena under scrutiny.

On the functions of background theories

In his book *Psychoanalysis at the Margins*, Paul Stepansky (2009) states that theoretical pluralism has become a "resting place"—the existence of several, more and less conflicting psychoanalytic theories has been commonly accepted in the psychoanalytic community. Stepansky is rather sceptical that psychoanalysis would get from the state of controversies and (cheap) theoretical pluralism to that of normal science, in which psychoanalytic knowledge would begin to cumulate—according to him certain ameliorative efforts to find common ground have indeed "stimulated a further round of animated controversy" (Stepansky, 2009, p. 213). I share Stepansky's pessimism, since considering that theories and explanations in general are always tied to certain viewpoints and interests, the plurality of psychoanalysis is by no means surprising.

Despite the diversity of psychoanalytic and other psychotherapeutic schools, psychotherapy *in general* is a very effective form of cure. In addition to this finding, consulting literature on psychotherapy research (for example, Cooper, 2008; Paris, 2008, pp. 23–30) informs us that in the current state of things it is problematic to argue that one form of psychotherapy were superior to others, and that we do not know what in psychotherapy cures.

Thus, talking-cure somehow affects the proxal causes of disorders, but similarly as there are lots of candidates for the causes of disorders, the curative aspects of psychotherapy may also be seen in many ways—for example, the working through of traumatic memories or relationships; operant conditioning; relationship with the therapist (empathy, corrective experience); becoming conscious of intrapsychic conflicts; cognitive shifting; or becoming able to recognise better one's feelings, desires, and fears.

Since disorders should be supposed to possess several necessary but not sufficient causes, talking-cure may be successful for many different reasons. In practice it is extremely difficult to show which of the causes the cure has affected.

> In summary, there is no direct cause-and-effect relationship between either biological or psychological factors and mental disorders. ... People become ill only when they suffer from temperamental vulnerability *and* are exposed to environmental

> stressors. This is why no theory exclusively based on biology (or psychology) can explain why people develop mental illnesses.
>
> (Paris, 2008, p. 9; emphasis in original)

It seems that one should not even conceive of presenting a complete, non-theory-laden explanation on the causes of disorders, or on the curative factors of psychotherapy.

The age-old Freud-wars directed us to think that the most important criterion for a theory is that it presents the cause(s) of disorders in a truthful manner—otherwise it could not direct a therapist towards correct interventions, since therapeutic techniques are always based on therapists' background theories. Joel Paris rephrases the critique I have presented above towards the Grünbaumian battlefield: "The problem with psychoanalysis is not that it is too complicated, but that it is too simple. ... As a therapy, its failures were rooted in grandiose claims, unsupported by data" (Paris, 2005, p. 156).

In his excellent book *Psychiatry in the Scientific Image*, Dominic Murphy (2006) studies the topics of this chapter. The dynamics between empirical study and clinical practice becomes nicely tightened in his statement: "The scientific project generalizes, whereas the clinical one uses the resources of the science to deal with particulars" (Murphy, 2006, p. 205). It seems that the Grünbaum-battle does not reach the core issues of psychotherapy and psychoanalysis, and even distorts the essence of psychotherapy. Thus, instead of thinking that psychoanalytic theories should present the causes of disorders, we should find an alternative way to conceptualise the criteria of plausible background theories of psychotherapy. Let us collect a list of the possible functions of and requirements for a scientific-enough background-theory of psychotherapy:

- There is a circular relationship between clinical theories and the techniques of psychotherapy—both shape the other. The most basic function of theories is to set the basic lines of clinical techniques and clinical practice. A therapist may have only rather vague hypotheses on the causes of clients' disorders, and how and why therapy might relieve them. Thus, theories should also direct therapists to focus on important topics (whatever they turn out to be). To put it in other words, theories should increase therapists' sensitivity to recognising the topics and kinds of interaction that may be crucial for the therapy. In a word, the nature of therapeutic technique should be *explorative.*

- Because both the causes of disorders and the phenomenal reality of clients are always idiosyncratic, a therapist should be good at imagining the personal dynamics of each person (see, for example, Reeder's (2004, pp. 37–52) sophisticated study). Reading theories and case studies presented in the psychotherapeutic literature enhances therapist's abilities in this respect, and that way he or she is able to make better therapeutic interventions. On this basis we might expect that it is favourable if a therapist is not restricted in his or her theoretical thinking.
- Sometimes psychotherapeutic relationships are very confusing and anxiety-provoking (also) for therapists. By sketching the dynamics of interaction on a theoretical level, theories enable therapists to cope with this aspect of their work.
- Background theories of a psychotherapy school should present formal models on the possible causal networks behind disorders and curative aspects of psychotherapy. Theories and models develop only if their strengths and weaknesses are studied in a systematic manner. In practice, this means that theories should be related to and compared with the up-to-date scientific views, and they should not contain non-necessary and groundless metaphysical presuppositions.

We get a more precise formulation on the last point by studying Murphy's views concerning explanations of psychiatry. He states:

> In trying to explain a mental disorder, we prescind from clinical variation across individual clients and treat the explanatory target as a process that unfolds the same way over and over again—a set of phenomena that usually occur together (the signs and symptoms) and that have a natural history (or course)—as a characteristic process that unfolds in a typical, though not wholly determinate, way.
>
> (Murphy, 2006, p. 205)

I think Murphy's view is very illuminative when considering what scientific-enough psychoanalytic theories might be. Let us see how he continues:

> To explain a mental disorder, then, is to explain an idealized picture of that disorder, to show what causes and sustains it, abstracted

> away from many of the details of its realization in individual clients. The detailed forms that pathologies take in individuals are the focus of clinical project, not the scientific one.
>
> (Murphy, 2006, p. 205)

Murphy calls these kinds of psychiatric theories *examplars*. Rosenberg (2000, p. 51), for his part, states that most ordinary and many scientific explanations are explanation sketches. There is no reason to presume psychoanalytic theories to be something more.

Conclusion

We can draw together the above considerations by stating that the main problem with psychoanalytic explanations is that both psychoanalytic folks and the critics of psychoanalysis possess too high expectations towards them. Currently there is no single explanation for any psychic disorder, no paradigm of research/treatment has created a wide-ranging and commonly accepted model on the causes of psychic disorders, and psychotherapy research is not able to tell neither the significance of therapist's background theory nor the curative factors of psychotherapy.

If one argues in this state of the art from either a pro or contra psychoanalysis position that the discipline should or can present causal explanations for disorders (perhaps even leaning on a single principle), it is legitimate to state that he or she has completely lost contact of the study having been put forward in the academic world.

During the past few decades there has been endless debates on what Freud actually meant, whether or not recent findings support his hundred-year-old hypotheses, and whether case studies may provide a basis for scientific models. I think it is time to take a leave of those discussions and in place re-orientate on the basis sketched in this chapter.

In the philosophy of science the boundaries of science are studied under the heading of "demarcation problem". Debates around the scientific standing of psychoanalysis reflect the presupposition that scientific endeavours are good, and the non-scientific ones dubious. In those debates the term "scientific" appears as a guarantee about something, or like a honorary title bestowed to distinguished efforts. However, this is a rather idealised conception of science (or, rather, of life). Namely, science has nothing to say about many extremely crucial issues of life like: Should I marry Sophia? Would I be happier with my life if I began to study medicine? Is Jimi Hendrix better with guitar than Ludwig Beethoven is on keyboards? Should I move to Houston? Would it make sense and life better if I practiced my golf swing for several hours a week?

There are at least two reasons why psychotherapy may be an affair that cannot be characterised as scientific—only *scientific enough*. First, since psychotherapy is closely related to values (philosophers tell us that it is impossible to deduce values from the facts), and second, since it is not possible to manage the huge amount of variables that affect psychotherapy (see Slife, 2004; Smith, 2009). Although psychotherapy could not be science or scientific, its background theories and methods may nevertheless lean more or less to the activities of science. Basically there are three requirements for a scientific-enough and practically adequate background theory of psychotherapy: it leans on academic study or at least does not contradict it; it directs therapists to act in such a manner that psychotherapy is useful for clients; and therapists can live with it. When a background theory aims at being something more, it is easily in conflict with prevailing views of research.

Above I left unexamined one important type of explanation, namely the mechanist explanation. The following chapter, written together with Juhani Ihanus, focuses on that.

CHAPTER FOUR

On the relation between neural and psychological mechanisms—neuropsychoanalysis and the "new mechanists"*

Vesa Talvitie and Juhani Ihanus

From its beginnings, neuropsychoanalysis has been a confusing enterprise. Neuroscience and psychoanalysis are different disciplines, using different terminology and methods and providing wholly different explanations. How, in this situation, might neuroscience verify or falsify psychoanalytic (and other psychological) theories, or contribute to their development? If it somehow succeeded in doing so, would this mean that psychological theories and entities would become reduced to neurophysiological ones? With such an outlook, the viewpoints of neuroscience are either irrelevant to psychoanalysis or will ultimately replace the psychological viewpoints.

In this chapter, the above dilemma is approached by focusing on "the new mechanism of neuroscience". This recent trend stresses that neurophysiological explanations are mechanistic explanations. From the psychoanalytic viewpoint, this is a highly interesting trend: since Freud, the nature and function of psychological mechanisms has been one of the core issues in psychoanalysis, and the relation between neural

---

*This chapter has originally been published in The Scandinavian Psychoanalytic Review (2011), 33: p. 130-141. Reproduced here with minor changes by the kind permission of the publisher.

and psychological mechanisms is surely an important matter when considering the significance of neuropsychoanalysis.

The idea of mechanisms behind behaviour and of mechanistic explanations for them can be traced back to at least the seventeenth century. In contemporary neuroscience, mechanistic explanations remain highly up to date. In the last five years William Bechtel and Carl Craver—the core figures of the "new mechanism" of the neurosciences and authors of recent books (Craver, 2007; Bechtel, 2008)—have argued that the essence of neuroscience is explaining matters by pinpointing neural mechanisms in particular. They claim that mechanistic explanations might provide a unifying framework for different explanations (Bechtel & Wright, 2009) and that "a multi-level mechanistic view of explanation" can bridge different levels and elaborate "a mosaic view of the unity of neuroscience" (Craver, 2007, p. 19). The endeavours of the mechanists also enable us to advance specific questions concerning the relation between psychological (psychodynamic) and neural mechanisms.

As far as we know, Craver's and Bechtel's ideas have not been studied in a neuropsychoanalytic context. Against this background, there is a need to place this new trend in neuroscience under closer scrutiny. In this study, defence mechanisms, which have a fundamental position in psychoanalytic theory (Freud, 1923b; A. Freud, 1936), serve as an example of a psychological mechanism.

The mechanistic approach in the behavioural sciences and the humanities

Many definitions of mechanistic explanation have been presented in neuroscience (see, e.g., Bechtel & Abrahamsen, 2005; Hedström, 2009; Machamer, Darden & Craver, 2000; Mahoney, 2003). According to Hedström (2009), a common characteristic among these definitions is that they describe in detail what gives rise to the regularities under scrutiny.

Descartes, whose arguments in favour of dualism are well known, also introduced mechanistic explanations of human behaviour. In his frame of thought, the soul is responsible for the deepest aspects of humaneness, but mechanistic explanations nevertheless cover many, rather complicated, activities: the beating of the heart and the system of the arteries; perceptual processes; the processing of sense-data in the imagination; memory; the movement of the limbs; reactions to food (depending on whether one is hungry or not); and the actions of walking and singing. Descartes' idea emerged from the fascination with different kinds of automata. (Cottingham, 1992; Hatfield, 1992)

A concrete idea of "a mechanism" can be formed by thinking of a machine or a device: the automatic speed control system of a car supposedly consists of sub-mechanisms such as different feedback loops. Evolutionary biology provides a more widespread viewpoint of the essence of mechanisms. Traits useful for survival and reproduction tend to become more common over the lifetime of a species. Biologists explain this by referring to the mechanism of natural selection. This mechanism cannot be pinpointed in the same way as the feedback loops of a car's speed control system. Instead, the mechanism can be revealed (or sketched) by studying the logic of evolution: if a trait improves the possibility of an organism to survive and reproduce, it probably reproduces more efficiently. In this way, nature "makes copies" of a trait for the next generation.

Like Descartes, the new mechanists and biologists talk about mechanisms. Mechanistic explanations have also been studied in the social sciences since the 1980s, Elster (1989, 1998) being a core figure. Elster's interest in mechanistic explanations emerges from the fact that in the social sciences generalisations cannot lead to laws, wherefore its theory risks becoming a recounting of scientific fables. Elster holds that mechanistic explanations created in the social sciences fall between law-like explanations and descriptions (Elster, 1998).

In the social sciences, mechanisms are often presented in terms of the so-called DBO theory (see Hedström, 2009), in which mechanisms are understood as a constellation of a person's Desires, Beliefs, and Opportunities. DBO theories are grounded on our propositional attitudes and on folk-psychology, studied in the first chapter. For example, a DBO theory may claim that the success of television shopping channels rests on the following mechanism: when people desire an easy way to lose weight, they are liable to believe in wonder diets of different kinds, and when an easy opportunity to try such a diet is presented, many will accept such a marvelous offer.

The "new mechanists" of neuroscience

One may be led to suppose that the new mechanists are fascinated with the computer metaphor and artificial intelligence, believe that humans are simply machines, advocate extremely reductionist views, and accept the tenets of eliminative materialism (according to which mental terms and entities can be reduced to neurophysiological ones). These suppositions are, however, erroneous. In order to understand the point of view of the new mechanists we must not think of computers but of *biological* mechanisms—life-preserving instincts or ego functions, the psychoanalyst would call them—that keep our body temperature constant, transfer properties from one generation to another, and guide birds' migration along the same route twice a year.

Bechtel (2008) and Craver (2007) address the mechanical essence of the explanations of neuroscience by studying issues such as memory, visual processing, the release of neurotransmitters, action potential, and the long-term potentiation of the synapses. Let us take a closer look at the first topic.

With memory we find that through the interplay between empirical research and clinical neuroscience, a large and scattered phenomenon has become clarified in a fine-grained manner. First, the general phenomenon of memory has been divided into several restricted domains: short-term, long-term, semantic, episodic, and procedural memory. Second, researchers have, largely, been able to localise these functions in different regions of the brain, which means that many neural components of memory competencies have been detected. Third (as a consequence of the second step), the focus is now on which activities each component structure of the brain supports and how successful memory performance is an outcome of an appropriate orchestration of those activities. In all, research has been able to reveal many central issues concerning the functions and effects of the neural mechanisms of memory.

In order to get the essence of mechanisms right, we must note that neurosurgeons cannot find the labels of mechanisms in the brain and that discrete mechanisms do not appear in distinct colours on a PET (Positron Emission Tomography) scan. Thus, neuroscientists do not *find* mechanisms, but *determine* them by showing which neural components, operations, and orchestrations or interactions give rise to a certain phenomenon.

Bechtel defines mechanism as: "a structure performing a function in virtue of its component parts, component operations, and their organization. The orchestrated functioning of the mechanism is responsible for one or more phenomena" (Bechtel, 2008, p. 13). For the new mechanists, a mechanistic explanation on a certain level contains three players or aspects: the *components* or parts; the *activities* that they perform; and their orchestration or *composition*.

Memory can be approached on different neural levels, and the mechanists hold that mechanisms form a hierarchy: a neural mechanism on one level is part of a mechanism on the next level. In the case of spatial memory, at the bottom of the mechanism hierarchy is the molecular level that consists of the mechanisms that "make the chemical and electrical activities of nerve cells possible". The next level is the cellular-electrophysiological one, the mechanisms that tell "how the hippocampus generates spatial maps". The mechanisms on the level of spatial formation have "computational properties of neural systems". The top level, spatial memory, too, can be seen as a mechanism as well as a part of the mechanisms of the next level, namely, the memory system at large. (Craver, 2007, pp. 165–170)

When arguing in favour of the mechanistic view, Bechtel and Craver are not calling for a revolution in neuroscience, but aim at show that good neuroscientific explanations actually pinpoint mechanisms.

Mechanisms in the psychoanalytic tradition

As a medical student in the 1870s, Freud was acquainted with the earlier mechanistic–materialistic research, for example, by du Bois-Reymond, Brücke, and Helmholtz and Ludwig (Gay, 1988; Sulloway, 1979). Of these researchers, he especially held in high and lifelong esteem his teacher and mentor Brücke, who saw nothing active within the organism other than the common physical-chemical forces. This was the intellectual background for the "Project": the function of mind was to be discerned and reduced to mechanical-physiological explanations. In "Project" Freud outlined many ideas, for example, how neurons (or the neural substrate) give rise to neuroses. In the current context, we might state that he tried to discern the neural mechanisms behind neuroses. One of the hardest problems, unsolved by Freud in "Project", was the riddle of defence and especially pathological repression. Freud had to abandon his ambition of developing a mechanical-neurophysiological explanation of defence (repression) and of the whole psychic apparatus. Clinical observation forced him to choose psychological rather than purely mechanical-neurophysiological explanations, although there remained the hope of one day finding a firmer basis for psychology in neurophysiology.

Already in the 1870s, there were doubts, even among the proponents of the (later-named) "Helmholtz School", concerning a purely mechanistic orientation in physiology and its reduction to physics and chemistry (Sulloway, 1979). At this time the phenomena—and the language—of psychology also began to attract the attention of researchers also in the field of natural sciences. Freud's letters to Fliess inform us that Freud renounced the neurological project in the beginning of 1896. On 16 March that year he wrote to Fliess: "I keep returning to psychology, I cannot escape its compelling call" (Masson, 1985, pp. 178–179), and he continued in a letter of 2 April: "As a young man I knew no longing other than for philosophical knowledge, and now I am about to fulfill it as I move from medicine to psychology" (Masson, 1985, p. 180).

In his first monograph, on aphasia, Freud (1891) had touched upon the mechanisms of memory and already investigated mental processes. Quite soon after that, in their preliminary communication, Freud and Breuer (1893) began to discuss the psychical mechanisms of hysterical phenomena (see also Freud, 1898b, on the psychical mechanism of forgetfulness). When considering Freud's shift from the neuroscientific viewpoint to the psychological one, however, the phrase "psychic apparatus" is crucial. In 1898, he mentioned the psychic apparatus, but—quite surprisingly—also the "sexual apparatus" (*Geschlechtsapparat*) (Freud, 1898a, p. 281). In "The interpretation of dreams" (Freud, 1900) he presented his view on the psychic apparatus in detail. He held that the essence of (the mechanisms of) the psychic apparatus could not be captured in terms of the natural science of his times, and so the psychic apparatus became a metapsychological concept (Talvitie & Ihanus, 2006).

Freud had already talked about defence (*Abwehr*) and the "neuropsychoses of defence" (*Abwehr-Neuropsychosen*) when collaborating with Breuer and Fliess (see the early discussion on defence and a theory of defence, Freud, 1894), and later he treated defences in particular as mechanisms (*Abwehrmechanismen*). At first, Freud (1896) held that defences are primarily directed against the drives and are aimed at maintaining the balance between their physical-chemical forces in the organism. The secondary defences were directed against symptoms (compromise formations between the drive impulses and the defences). Later, having created his structural model, he thought that there are also defences (of the ego) enabling one to deal with conflicts and anxiety (Freud, 1926).

When trying to capture the role of mechanisms in general and the relation between the neural and psychic mechanisms in Freud's thinking, we can say that the "Project" is about neural mechanisms and the neural apparatus. However, according to Sulloway (1979, pp. 122–131), in the "Project" Freud was not exclusively in favour of physical-chemical ("mechanical") reduction but also endorsed organismic-evolutionary ("biological") explanations. Later, he focused on the psychic mechanisms in terms of the psychic apparatus, defences, and the ego, all considered as a group of psychic mechanisms.

There are many images of Freud as a scientist. He was a neurologist (trained especially in neurophysiology and neuropathology), but he is most often seen as one of the greatest psychologists. Sulloway entitled his book *Freud, Biologist of the Mind: Beyond the Psychoanalytic Legend.* As late as 1933, Freud concluded that "strictly speaking" there are only two disciplines: psychology (sociology being part of "applied psychology") and the natural science (Freud, 1933, p. 179). Freud himself tended to downplay his neurological side by, for example, not including his pre-psychoanalytic (neuroscientific) works in the *Gesammelte Schriften* (*Collected Works*). The common distinction between the humanities and the natural sciences has helped keep psychological, neurophysiological, and biological aspects of psychoanalysis separate.

As to mechanisms, post-Freudian psychoanalysis has not developed notable insights into the relation between the neural and psychological mechanisms—only neuropsychoanalysis has faced the challenge of integrating these.

The new mechanists' project and neuropsychoanalysis

Even though the new mechanists have not paid attention to neuropsychoanalysis—we can imagine the criticism they would present towards it—some neuroscientists have shown an interest in the neural correlates of "psychoanalytic phenomena", and some psychoanalytic researchers have studied neural counterparts for phenomena such as dreams (Yu, 2003), affective reactions (Watt, 2003), and even creativity (Oppenheim, 2005). However, there is little or no interest in describing in detail the neural mechanisms behind these phenomena. Reporting a parallel "what-might-happen-in-the-brain-at-the-same-time story" of a psychological phenomenon is not an explanation. Such a story is not necessarily even interesting—already in Descartes' times people presumed that psychological matters possess neural counterparts. As an illustration, let us sketch how the new mechanists might approach "the return of the repressed" and transference.

Psychoanalysts have found that repressed ideas and impulses may appear in a metaphorical or symbolic form in a dream or as a slip of the tongue. A detailed description of how the brain gives rise to these phenomena needs to include identifying the neural mechanisms behind them. That task can be divided into several sub-tasks, for example, to define how repressed ideas are represented by the brain, or what a (repressed) impulse of the id is in neuroscientific terms; how the brain detects the need for repression; and to explain how the brain creates the metaphorical form of an idea or a wish. When we have precise answers to these questions, a mechanistic explanation has been formed.

With transference, the sub-tasks would be something as follows: to show how the early object relations are represented by the brain; to show what makes the brain detect a match between the current object relation and the earlier one, and how it actually manages to do it; and to define how the brain executes the transference reactions and hides their inappropriateness from the subject's awareness.

It seems that from the perspective of neuropsychoanalysis, the new mechanists' project is perfectly reasonable: behind the patterns of subjective reactions and experiences there are not only neural correlates, but also neural mechanisms, and one should try to pinpoint them in detail. At the same time, the project is also extremely challenging. One might think that neuropsychoanalysis will never be able to stand up to join the new mechanists in their challenge—the neural basis of the "psychoanalytic phenomena" is often considered not possible to present with such preciseness. We understand the underlying ideas of this attitude as the following:

- The neural mechanism in question is complex, that is, it is composed of several parts that are distributed in multiple regions of the brain, and the current (and possibly also future) tools of neuroscience cannot capture such complexity.
- Psychoanalytic observations and models are not exact enough to determine neural mechanism.
- The phenomenon or property under scrutiny is multi-realised (or over-determined: see Waelder, 2007), that is, it has different neural correlates in different persons, and thus a single mechanism cannot be pinpointed.

How do psychodynamic or psychological mechanisms then fit into the mechanists' picture? As mentioned, Bechtel and Craver claim that neural mechanisms form a hierarchy where a lower-level mechanism is a component of a higher level one. If we think of psychological mechanisms as being at the top of the hierarchy, should we then assume that when we have come to explain a certain phenomenon in terms of a psychological mechanism we need to continue by determining the neural mechanisms that underlie it?

Bechtel has written articles about the essence of psychology and psychological explanation (Bechtel, 2005; Bechtel & Wright, 2009; Wright & Bechtel, 2007), and his ideas might help us figure out the relation between neurophysiological and psychological domains, and neural and psychological mechanisms. His psychology is, however, different from that of the psychoanalysts. In the article "What is psychological explanation?" (Bechtel & Wright, 2009), the representatives of psychology are psychophysiology, physiological psychology, and information-processing psychology. The topics of personality, psychopathology, and developmental and clinical psychology, among others, are missing. In short, Bechtel and Wright leave out the psychology of personal, idiosyncratic issues.

Considering that psychoanalysis focuses on personal issues and subjective experience in particular, psychoanalysts and the new mechanists seem to live in wholly different landscapes. The possible benefit of the new mechanism of neuroscience for neuropsychoanalysis can be reached only after the implications of this discrepancy on psychology have been made clear. Zachar's (2000) view of the essence of psychology (or the nature of *psychological* research) is of help here.

Approaching the relation between neuroscience and pyschoanalysis through Zachar's "three anchors of psychology"

Zachar defines psychology through the following three "anchors":

- Psychology is interested in why individuals differ—why, for example, one person frequently uses certain defence mechanisms, while another rarely does so.
- Psychology studies both what takes place in one's "head" (mind and brain) as well as what takes place in a person's environment.

This perspective defines psychology in relation to sociology and behaviourism, both of which focus on the outer world. In addition, it alerts us to the difference between psychology and psychoanalysis on the one side and neuroscience on the other—the latter focusing solely on the brain and for the most part leaving unexamined what sense-data tells us about the outer world.

- Psychology is not interested only in detached psychic and neural processes and states but also in their interrelations—one's whole self.

The first anchor: the human species and the individual

As to the first anchor, the new mechanists study species-specific properties and are not interested in individual differences (something that holds also for many other branches of neuroscience). Contrary to this, psychoanalysts focus on personal matters in particular—patterns of experiencing, psychic disorders, creativity, and human suffering, to mention just a few areas. Idiosyncratic features are determined by, and sometimes throw light on, species-specific features, but it is nevertheless justifiable to state that the objects of study of the new mechanism and psychoanalysis are different.

To follow Bermúdez's terminology, we can claim that psychoanalysts seek *horizontal explanations* that aim at explaining "a particular event or state in terms of distinct (and usually temporally antecedent) events or states" (Bermúdez, 2005, pp. 31–33). Neuroscientists are interested in *vertical explanations* that try to reach the neurophysiological basis of the state of things.

A distinction between the "personal" and "subpersonal" levels of explanation (Bermúdez, 2005, pp. 27–35) is closely related to this issue. Neuroscientists in general and the new mechanists in particular typically focus on the subpersonal level: they explain phenomena by referring to the activity (activations) of the parts of human organisms, that is, of certain regions of the brain. Personal-level explanations are based on the entities or properties that characterise man (or woman) as a whole—people's beliefs, fears, and desires. In Bermúdez (2005, pp. 35–37) we also find a phrase—"the interface problem"—for the core challenge of neuropsychoanalysis: What is the interface between psychological (personal-level) and neurophysiological (subpersonal-level) terminologies and theories?

The second anchor: the mind/brain and the environmental context

The second anchor makes visible another difference between the new mechanists' and psychoanalysts' interests: when studying a function of the brain, for example, memory, the mechanists silently presume that there is an outer world about which one makes perceptions that are personally relevant to the perceiving subject, who also retains and recalls different kinds of memories. In laboratory studies, the variables are generally controlled as far as possible, and thus the environment lacks the richness of our normal surroundings. In the laboratory, subjects process *data*, and researchers are usually uninterested in the subjects' personal signification of the stimuli—behaviour is studied in a narrow context. (Bechtel, 2008; Peressini, 1997)

Psychoanalysis, for its part, describes (in rich detail) a person's phenomenal internal reality as well as his or her surroundings. Psychoanalysts do not only study the meanings of the sense-data, but also fantasies, symbols, and metaphors, and one's interaction with the world from a wide-ranging temporal perspective. The third anchor articulates the difference of interests between neuroscience and psychoanalysis even further.

The third anchor: the self and the multi-realisation of mental properties

The third anchor states that psychological study is characterised by an interest in the person's total self, that is, in the interaction between his or her memories, beliefs, desires, feelings, and so on. This reflects the essence of psychoanalytic interest, too: contrary to neuroscience and laboratory research in general, in psychoanalysis a person's reactions and mental states are not studied in isolation. Instead, they are related to one another as well as to the subject's personal history and fantasies. This issue has a bearing on whether or not we are able to determine neural correlates for the "psychoanalytic" phenomena or neural mechanisms for them. Let us explore this question through the idea of the multi-realisation of mental properties.

Cummins (1983, 2000) defines the essence of psychology by arguing that psychic functions are multi-realised in the brain. The idea of multi-realisation is illustrated by referring to the functions of clocks and tin openers, among others. Measuring time, the function of a clock, is not dependent on the physical properties of clocks: a clock may be analogical or digital, and it can be based on, for example, the streaming of water or sand. Moreover, in the heyday of the computer metaphor, it was often said that psychic functions, for example, the recognition of objects and different kinds of memory, can be understood by the analogy with a computer.

A core idea of multi-realisation in psychology is that the location of the psychic functions in the human brain varies: although two persons perform the same task or are in the same situation (counting, playing chess, trying to recall a list of words), different areas of each person's brain may be active. Let us put it in a different way: the multi-realisation of a psychological quality or characteristic means that there is a shared behavioural or phenomenal pattern (e.g., a certain defence, an exceptional talent in chess, or a psychic disorder) without a shared neurophysiological basis.

Cummins' claim about multi-realisation laid the ground for the autonomy of psychology—psychological functions cannot be equated with certain parts of the brain. Some researchers have criticised Cummins' claim, and recently Aizava and Gillett (2009) have questioned that critique. We contend that the new mechanists do not deny multi-realisation, but would like to challenge it as far as possible (Bechtel, 2008; Craver, 2007). The debate on multi-realisation runs on a very abstract and general level, and, when applied to psychology, focuses on species-specific properties. We summarise the debate by stating that it cannot be ruled out that species-specific properties are multi-realised.

Contrary to species-specific properties, the development of, for example, defence mechanisms, is strongly affected by the individual's unique genetic constitution or temperament as well as by his or her unique life history. For this reason, it is likely that there is also considerable inter-individual variance in the neural counterparts of defences.

Zachar's third anchor implies the multi-realisation of personal properties from another angle: psychoanalysis focuses on the complex dynamics of desires, fears, memories, fantasies, etc. (i.e., on the self), and complexity is surely characteristic of the neural counterparts of such dynamics, too. When two basically similar complex systems (humans) develop in different environments, their inner dynamics become different. Thus, behind the personal characteristics that emerge in the interaction with the environment in the long term, there are *idiosyncratic* neural dynamics. In fact, the clinical phenomena that the psychoanalytic models aim to explain—psychic problems such as depression, schizophrenia, and borderline personality disorder—are considered to be multi-realised (Mitchell, 2008; Murphy, 2008; Schaffner, 2008).

For us, the core question is whether psychological mechanisms, for example, defences, are multi-realised: Do all people using a certain defence have a shared neural structure, or do neural correlates of the defence have inter-individual variance?

Modell (2003, p. 56) claims: "Splitting-off or dissociation and repression are usually described as different defense 'mechanisms,' but instead, these different defense 'mechanisms' may simply reflect individual differences." Consider the fact that after the times of Galileo Galilei millions of people deceived themselves that the world is flat and has a special place in the centre of the solar system. Did they share a neural mechanism that could be localised in the brain? Did they share neural properties with those who deny the existence of Nazi concentration camps?

We must presume that the answer is negative—the considerations above give us good reasons to think that the neural counterparts of defences are characterised by complex neural dynamics and contain considerable inter-individual variance (i.e., they are multi-realised). Thus, it is not especially surprising that Northoff and Boeker (2006) assume that defence mechanisms are "complex modes of emotional-cognitive interaction" (Northoff & Boeker, 2006, p. 70) and do not even try to localise them in the brain. Instead, they hypothesise that defences can be approached from the neurophysiological viewpoint in terms of "coordination and adjustment of neuronal activity across multiple brain regions" (Northoff & Boeker, 2006, p. 70).

Zachar's anchors amount to, first, that psychoanalysis and neuroscience not only approach the same issues from different levels, but possess wholly different perspectives on human beings. Second, it seems clear that the essential requirement of the new mechanists cannot be fulfilled: we are unable to describe the neural mechanism behind defences *in detail*.

Bechtel (2007) holds that the autonomy of psychological explanations in general is due to the fact that neuroscience cannot treat either the complex dynamics of the mind/brain or those of the environment (see also, e.g., Bem, 2001; Looren de Jong & Schouten, 2007). Bechtel and Wright (2009) admit that in complex neural dynamics, the basic building-blocks of mechanistic explanations (neural component parts, operations, organisation) are difficult to apply. Thus, we suppose that with defence mechanisms the new mechanists would abstain from their claim to determine in detail the neural mechanisms behind them.

The bearable lightness of being interdisciplinary

It seems that we must admit that psychoanalysis and neuroscience are simply different undertakings, and that there is no simple code or logic that would reveal the relation between the explanations provided by each discipline. Some present-day neuroscientists (e.g., Andreasen, 2001) and philosophers (Bickle, 2003) support reductionist lines of thought. However, the idea that neuroscientific explanations are somehow more foundational than psychological ones is currently seen as problematic in the philosophy of psychology (see, e.g., Schouten & Looren de Jong, 2007) as well as that of psychiatry (Kendler & Parnas, 2008). Instead, a pluralism of explanations is commonly favoured. Thus, the reductionist dream of anchoring psychoanalytic models to biology and neuroscience appears to reflect Kantian metaphysics (see Talvitie & Ihanus, 2011b), positivistic ideals of twentieth century, or more recent aims of eliminative materialism.

In the case of defence and other psychological mechanisms, this conclusion implies that psychological mechanisms cannot be reduced to neural mechanisms and that the existence of a psychological mechanism cannot be confirmed by identifying the neural mechanisms behind it. Nor is an explanation in terms of neural mechanisms more foundational than an explanation referring to psychological mechanisms.

There are, however, still good reasons to study psychoanalytic issues from the perspective of neuroscience. We cannot deny the intimate connection between the mind and the brain and bypass the fact that in many cases neuroscientific perspectives have been proven to be useful when creating psychological models. The neuroscientists' job remains to search neural correlates and mechanisms behind different phenomena, regardless of the practical significance of the findings. Psychoanalysts should be alert to the progress taking place in the domain of neuroscience—in some cases it surely contains relevance to the development of psychoanalytic models. We just do not have a method of forecasting in which cases that relevance will be found.

Benjamin Rubinstein (1997) wrote that psychoanalytic theoretical terms are *proto-neurophysiological*: they cannot be reduced to neurophysiological terms, yet they should not contradict the views of neuroscience. When considering the scientific status of psychoanalytic theories, we should not underestimate the significance of proto-neurophysiology or "speculative neurology" (Edelman & Tononi, 2000, p. 178). Below, we will present a conception of defence mechanisms that might be called "holistic". It illustrates how psychoanalysis might—we think should—amalgamate the views of neuroscience and other disciplines to its own thinking.

Although the term "holistic" has connotations of new-age jargon, in philosophy, holism is connected both to meaning structures (e.g., of words) and to the testing of scientific hypotheses. In both cases, holism refers to the claim that in order to study a part (the meaning of a word or the truth-value of a hypothesis), the part has to be set in an appropriate, *whole* context (a sentence or a scientific theory) (see Godfrey-Smith, 2003).

In their article "Thinking about mechanisms", Machamer, Darden, and Craver write:

> Higher-level entities and activities are thus essential to the intelligibility of those at lower levels, just as much as those at lower levels are essential for understanding those at higher levels. It is the integration of different levels into productive relations that renders the phenomenon intelligible and thereby explains it.
>
> (Machamer, Darden & Craver 2000, p. 23)

In the spirit of these authors we argue that neuropsychoanalysis should form a holistic view of defence mechanisms by interrelating the viewpoints of clinical psychoanalysis, the new mechanists, empirical psychological research (see Hassin, Uleman & Bargh 2005), psychological models (Mele, 2001), and that of speculative neuroscience (Edelman & Tononi, 2000; LeDoux, 1998).

A holistic conception of the defence mechanism: operations, components, and orchestration

When considering a defence, the foundational issue is that there is something against which it operates; psychological defences serve keeping something out of consciousness. For a clinician, it is perhaps enough to think of the function, triggering, and outcomes of a defence. The new mechanists' way of thinking leads us to also ask about its constituent parts. Applying Bechtel (2005), we can sketch the following five operations (or aspects) as constituting a defence mechanism.

The first operation concerns the threat that a person does not wish to face. In classical psychoanalysis, the danger is usually seen as deriving from an impulse of the id that leads to internal conflict. Modell (2003) claims that the unconscious is a source of danger in itself: "It is the intensity of excitation itself that poses the danger" (Modell, 2003, p. 54). In terms of the new mechanists' logic, one could proceed with this Freudian conception by determining the neural parts of the defence mechanism—how the danger is represented by the brain. If we hold that the threat lies in the domain of the mental unconscious, that aim is, of course, senseless.

The second operation is the detection of the threat and the triggering of the defence. Regardless of whether the threat is coded in the brain or lies in the mental unconscious, present-day neuroscience and empirical study open up a way to comprehend the activation of a defence mechanism: we perceive (potentially) dangerous matters all the time, and our perceptions activate inner threats—there are stimuli that are signs of danger. The crucial thing is that according to current views, *we are able to detect dangers unconsciously*. Furthermore, the detection may trigger rather sophisticated neural routines that enable the avoidance of the danger without conscious planning. LeDoux (1998), Edelman (Edelman & Tononi, 2000), and the researchers talking about "the new unconscious" (Hassin, Uleman & Bargh, 2005), among others, have studied these matters, and it is not necessary to introduce their findings here (for a more comprehensive study, see Talvitie, 2009, and Talvitie & Ihanus, 2002). The important thing is that the rather bold psychoanalytic idea about the unconscious functioning of the defences is currently supported by studies carried out within several paradigms of psychology and neuroscience.

The third operation, the selection of the defence, has two dimensions. Reflecting Zachar's first anchor, what is selected depends on the subject's personal characteristics: if an individual is verbal and intelligent, he or she is liable to use intellectualisation; an artist may project inner conflicts into their paintings or stories, and so on. In addition, and reflecting closely the second anchor, the selection depends on the situation. Each environmental context supports the use of certain defences and makes the use of others more difficult. When a certain threat is recognised, either on the psychoanalytic couch, at a party, or on a building site, a different defence mechanism is "selected". In his review article, Rofé (2008) concludes that even repression (or amnesia caused by a trauma) is highly context-dependent.

The fourth operation is the factual functioning of the defence, that is, how the defence mechanism hides the threat from the person. This issue is illustrated below in the case of Sam.

Billig (1999) compels us to presume a fifth operation: a blocked topic must not be followed by silence, so a replacement topic is needed. According to him, defences are less "acts" (possessing localisable neural counterparts) and more ways of thinking and approaching the world—repression "is a way of saying to oneself 'talk, or think, of this, not that'" (Billig, 1999, p. 54).

A successful orchestration means that the defence mechanism is able to distort reality in a way that is acceptable to the individual. In the case presented below, this means that Sam's trust in Sally's faithfulness does not wobble and that he keeps his anxiety at bay and is able to deal with his everyday life in a comfortable enough way.

Defence mechanism illustrated

In order to comprehend parts, components, and orchestration on a more concrete level, and to see how an interdisciplinary approach enables us to create a fuller view of the essence of a defence mechanism, let us study an example taken outside of the psychoanalytic tradition. Self-deception is a ubiquitous feature of defence and repression. Mele's work *Self-deception Unmasked* (2001) is a significant recent contribution from a cognitivist viewpoint. He illustrates self-deception through the following example:

> Sam has believed for many years that his wife, Sally, would never have an [extramarital] affair. In the past, his evidence for this proposition was quite good. Sally obviously adored him, she never displayed a sexual interest in another man, she condemned extramarital sexual activity, she was secure, she was happy with her family life, and so on. However, things recently began to change.

> Sally is now arriving home late from work on the average of two nights a week, she frequently finds excuses to leave the house alone after dinner and on weekends, and Sam has been informed by a close friend that Sally has been seen in the company of a certain Mr. Jones at a theater and local lounge. Nevertheless, Sam continues to believe that Sally would never have an affair. But he is wrong. Her relationship with Jones is by no means platonic.
>
> (Mele, 2001, p. 57)

In psychoanalytic terms, Mele describes here the defence mechanism of denial. In order to examine the elements of the mechanism, let us consider first the essence and representation of the threat (*the first operation of a defence mechanism*). A cognitivist like Mele might say that Sam is repressing the *possibility* that Sally is having an affair. However, there are varieties of other fitting, more or less theoretical, descriptions of what is threatening Sam: unbearably strong feelings of sorrow and rage, the violation of his self-image as a manly and interesting man, and the loss of an idealised object. Here we face, again, limitations due to multi-realisability and complex psychological as well as neural dynamics: we can only speculate on how the threat is represented by the brain.

Regardless of which of these descriptions we choose, we should consider whether Sam detected the threat unconsciously (the possibility that Sally is having an affair did not appear in his consciousness), consciously (he is ready to state, "Of course that may mean that she is having an affair, but I just don't think Sally would do a thing like that"), or both ways (*the second operation*). In any case, anyone having an intact brain is able to deduct that the details of Sally's recent behaviour imply the possibility that she is having an affair. Thus, the challenge is to tell how Sam succeeded in not doing that or in not taking the threat seriously: Which are the defence operations that in effect hide the threat?

If we consider the selection of the defence mechanism (*the third operation*), the question is: Why has denial in particular been selected? On one side, there are Sam's personal characteristics. If he had been more inclined to create abstract ideas, he might have turned to sublimation instead of denial by beginning to think of an open relationship as representing the highest form of closeness between two people. On the other side, there is the context: if Sam's friend had told him about Mr. Jones when they were drunk in a bar, the mechanism of acting out might have been triggered; Sam might have hit his friend for insulting Sally in such a rude manner. The selection of a defence mechanism is like throwing a loaded dice on a ragged surface—neuroscience may tell us more or less about the dice (the behavioural dispositions of Sam's brain), but nothing about the surface (the signs, social conventions, moral codes, symbols, and metaphors embedded in one's current environment).

As to the defence mechanism's capacity to hide the threat from awareness (*fourth operation*), Mele talks about "processes that contribute to motivationally biased beliefs, including beliefs that people are self-deceived in acquiring" (Mele, 2001, p. 25). Mele suggests several processes/operations through which the threat remains hidden for Sam, for example, *the positive misinterpretation of data* ("[I]f Sally were having an affair she would want to hide it and that her public meetings with Jones consequently indicate that she is *not* sexually involved with him" (p. 57; emphasis in original), *the negative misinterpretation of data* (downplaying evidence in favour of Sally's infidelity), *selective focusing* (attending to matters implying Sally's faithfulness and not attending to matters referring to an affair between Sally and Mr. Jones), and *selective evidence gathering* (conducting investigations that probably will not reveal the affair and not conducting more effective investigations).

The *fifth operation*—that of saying to oneself "talk, or think, of this, not that"—means that Sam does not slow down to reflect on his true feelings and the logic of his thought processes. If someone confronted his beliefs concerning Sally, Sam would make jokes and quickly turn the discussion to other topics.

In conclusion, the new mechanists' conception of psychological defence enables us to depict its structure in terms of parts, operations, and orchestration. Through this we are also able to perceive the issues that neuropsychoanalysis should put forward in a more or less speculative manner. Non-psychoanalytic psychologists' and neuroscientists' current views of unconscious processing thus provide considerable support for the psychoanalytic idea of the unconscious functioning of the defences. Mele's model and his example of self-deception, for its part, shed light on the selection of a defence and the psychological micro-processes (or operations) behind them. Machamer and Sytsma (2007) argue in favour of a multi-level approach by stating: "[I]n order to refine our scientific explanations ... we need to move up, then down, and again up the levels to coordinate what we find at one level of the mechanism with what we have assumed at another" (Machamer &

Sytsma, 2007, p. 212). A holistic basic orientation of this kind provides a foundation for a genuine interdisciplinary collaboration.

Concluding discussion

The new mechanists' advice to neuropsychoanalysis might be that one should not be so fascinated with the general stories about the neural correlates, but instead focus on neural and psychological mechanisms. However, at least in the case of the neural mechanisms behind defences, that advice cannot be followed. There is no reason to blame the psychoanalytic models or methods of study for this. The new mechanists are able to identify neural mechanisms behind memory, because they focus on the matters common to a whole species, but psychoanalysts study complex idiosyncratic phenomena.

The difference between the neuroscientists' and the psychoanalysts' interests can be compared to those of the criminologists and the detectives; the former aim at gathering general knowledge in their domain, whereas the latter apply whatever knowledge may help to puzzle out the unique case at hand. For detectives/psychoanalysts there are no simple rules on how to apply to their unique cases the knowledge provided by criminologists or neuroscientists.

The more general conclusion to be drawn may be that the relation between the neural and the psychological cannot be expressed in a simple and straightforward manner. Although neuropsychoanalytic studies usually do not focus on the issue (Modell, 2003, being a notable exception), there is a tension in neuropsychoanalysis between natural science and the humanities. Neuropsychoanalysis seems to wish to have it both ways: enjoying the fruits of (hard) science without losing contact with the hermeneutics of clinical practice.

After Freud, psychoanalysis has tended to shun scientific, reductionist lines of thought. However, the hope that neuroscience might be of help in validating psychoanalytic ideas appears to imply something at least close to reductionism. If neuroscience were not foundational, how would it even be considered to verify or falsify psychological models that have been presented by psychoanalysis? We propose a more modest conception of interdisciplinarity: when a holistic model of a phenomenon under scrutiny is put forward, psychoanalytic viewpoints can become interconnected to mainstream views while nonetheless preserving their identity.

CHAPTER FIVE

The unconscious, the brain, and self-consciousness—on psychoanalytic metaphysics

When the scientific status of psychoanalysis is considered, metaphysical ideas behind the discipline cannot be overlooked. According to Michael Loux (2008, p. x) there are two conventional ways to define metaphysics. Immanuel Kant held that metaphysics studies topics such as the nature of God, the problem of free will, and the nature of the mind. An older, Aristotelian definition, suggests that the object of study is being, and thus metaphysics is the most foundational and general branch of study. A decade or two ago metaphysics was seen as a somewhat old-fashined topic among philosophers. Recently, however, there has been renewed interest towards it.

I think the above, rather inexact definitions, are enough for the purposes of this chapter—below we will put certain foundational aspects of psychoanalysis under scrutiny. Freud himself made the link between meta*physics* and his own meta*psychological* model. However, I will not approach the topic from that perspective. Instead, I will focus on three interwoven parts of Freud's thinking: first, his views on the mental unconscious, second, the relation between the unconscious and the brain, and third, the Freudian view of the nature of introspection (or (self-)consciousness). Again, it is appropriate to study

Freud's views in particular since here psychoanalysis still leans on his thinking. It is also appropriate to focus on the above three issues since psychoanalytic folks *not* accepting, for example, the Freudian metapsychology, nevertheless use an approach to the unconscious and introspection in a Freudian way.

Freud's philosophical background

Freud's thinking is an idiosyncratic mixture of nineteenth-century German romanticism and early twentieth-century positivism. When it comes to the first, Freud studied in the latter part of the nineteenth century, views of such idealistic philosophers as Immanuel Kant and G. W. F. Hegel were still commonly favoured. The picture was not radically different during the first half of the twentieth century, and thus from the perspective of a history of ideas it is rather natural that the Freudian theory postulates non-conscious entities and agents into the mind. (Galdston, 1956; Tauber, 2010)

Mature Freud kept silent about his philosophical ideas, but in his youth, Freud was *very* interested in philosophy, and behind his theories we do find a certain kind of philosophy. There is enough evidence (for example, Fichtner, 1992, pp. 233–234; Freud, 1915, p. 171; Fulgencio, 2005, p. 109; Tauber, 2010, pp. 116–128) to hold that Freud leaned on Kantian metaphysics—for him the unconscious was (like) *das Ding an sich*, which cannot be observed.

Positivism emerged in the beginning of the twentieth century on the grounds created by Auguste Comte (in the nineteenth century), Ernst Mach, and early ("Tractatus"-) Ludwig Wittgenstein. The positivists' project was to safeguard the reliability of scientists' findings by restricting to observational data. Their stand towards metaphysics was negative: science should not speculate on metaphysical issues. (Godfrey-Smith, 2003, pp. 19–38)

Freud became fascinated by the empiricistic spirit of positivism, and even signed together with Albert Einstein and Mach the call for the foundation of a "Society for Positivist Philosophy" in 1912. The call was published in both *Physikalische Zeitschrift* and *Zentralblatt für Psychoanalyse* (Fulgencio, 2000, 2005; Smith, 1999; Tauber, 2010). Considering positivists' stance towards metaphysical considerations, it is difficult to comprehend from the present-day perspective how Freud was able to both support positivism and keep metapsychological/-physical speculations at the core of psychoanalytic theorising.

The mind, "ordinary mentalism", and "psychoanalytic mentalism"

Rène Descartes prominently suggested that the body and the mind are distinct substances. The former is a material machinery, whereas the latter is non-material substance lacking extensions. Philosophers have been in pains with Descartes' conception for almost four centuries. Cartesian (substance-) dualism is difficult to advocate, and during the past few decades mainstream philosophy of mind has tended to downgrade or even deny the mental in order to save the materialistic worldview. Materialistic philosophers have been eager to argue that mental matters are, in one way or another, actually or basically physical ones.

Excluding some philosophers, it is evident for everybody that humans possess pains and pleasures, and that each of us has a stream of consciousness containing feelings and mental images of different kinds. The mind has been equated with phenomenal consciousness, and Strawson (1994) argues that the mental actually should be anchored to phenomenal matters. Everybody agrees that the brain causes or at least affects our experiences and behaviour, and *ordinary mentalism*—as we babtised the standpoint in Talvitie and Ihanus (2011b)—holds that our conscious desires, fears, and decision are able to do that too. The tension between this kind of folk-psychology and materialism was treated in the second chapter.

In *The Freudian Unconscious and Cognitive Neuroscience: From Uunconscious Fantasies to Neural Algorithms* (Talvitie, 2009, pp. 17–44) I introduced the origins of some the most common mental terms. The lesson was that the mental terms (for example, "mind", "geist", "soul", and "psyche") have different origins and connotations, and it should not be thought that they simply were synonyms, sharing the same point of reference. Philosophers that "take mind and mental matters serisously" stress that the mind should not be considered an entity, a substance, a "thing", or a sphere, but an aspect of the human. Such a line of thought leads to, for example, the following characterisations and definitions: "[C]onsciousness is a feature of the brain ... consciousness is a state the brain can be in, in the way that liquity and solidity are states that water can be in" (Searle, 2008, p. 56); "To have a mind is to have an intellect and rational will. It is to be able to reason, to apprehend things as deliberate, decide or choose what to do or believe, and to modify one's feelings and attitudes, in the light of reasons" (Hacker, 2010, p. 256); "Having a mind isn't like having brown eyes or a sore elbow .... To say that something 'has a mind' is to classify it as a certain sort of thing capable of certain characteristic sorts of behaviors and functions (sensation, percepetion, memory, learning, reasoning, consciousess, action, and the like)" (Kim, 1998, p. 5).

There is no doubt that psychoanalysis falls on the side of mentalism. However, it is very different from the ordinary mentalism, and thus we (Talvitie & Ihanus, 2011b) talked about *psychoanalytic mentalism*. In the core of it we find the idea that the mind consists of unconscious and conscious parts—in addition to phenomenal consciousness, also (some) unconscious matters are held to be mental. This claim is extremely complicated and also problematic.

Terms are conventions concerning the use of language, and we might think that psychoanalytic folks just use mental terms differently from ordinary mentalists. However, below I will make clear the case that in the scope of psychoanalysis the claim that the unconscious is mental is not seen merely as linguistic innovation—it is thought to reflect the true nature of the human.

Analysts often even define the identity of psychoanalysis through the mental unconscious: other psychological disciplines focus on behaviour and/or consciousness, whereas the object of study of psychoanalysis is the unconscious. Thus, terminological and metaphysical nitpicking around the unconscious is by no means irrelevant. It may be the case that a considerable part of the disagreements between psychoanalysis and other branches of study can be tracked to the domain of metaphysics.

The Freudian proof for the existence of the unconscious

Freud likes to use metaphors and rhetorical tricks. That should not let hide the fact that he does not present any idea or guess on how the mental unconscious might exist. I think Freud's statements like the following have led psychoanalytic thinking rather seriously astray:

> To most people who have been educated in philosophy the idea of anything psychical which is not also conscious is so

> inconceivable that it seems to them absurd and refutable simply by logic. I believe this is only because they have never studied the relevant phenomena of hypnosis and dreams, which—quite apart from pathological manifestations—necessitate this view. Their psychology of consciousness is incapable of solving the problems of dreams and hypnosis.
>
> (Freud, 1923b, p. 13)

Thus, according to psychoanalytic mentalism, the phenomena mentioned should be seen as proving the existence of the unconscious.

Dreams, hypnosis, and psychic disorders all happen to have been explained in the history of humankind by referring to God and other supernatural matters. From the Old Testament we remember the story about the pharaoh's dream about seven fat cows and seven gaunt cows, which Joseph was able to interpret. In the Christian tradition, we also often meet the idea that God communicates his will through dreams. Psychic disorders have been seen as caused by evil, and thus exorcists and religious healers have cured them. Phenomena we currently set under the heading hypnosis were also previously given religious interpretations, and not until the middle of the nineteenth century did Franz Mesmer pull it from the region of religion to that of research.

We can also see the similarity between certain psychoanalytic lines of thought and those presented by the advocates of intelligent design (ID). At the core of intelligent design-thinking is the idea that the traits of animals and plants are so expedient that they cannot have been developed "by accident" (i.e., through the logic of evolution). Similarly, in terms of psychoanalytic mentalism, in dreams, slips, symbolic relationships between distinct matters, and other clinical phenomena we find such an order, systematicy, and sense, which cannot have been produced by the neural networks of the brain. Thus, according to the psychoanalytic logic, the characteristics of dreams, slips, and disorders provide proof for the existence of some kind of "designer(s)"— mental apparatus, censorship, the three agents of the structural model, and repressed contents.

The crucial thing here is that religious and psychoanalytic explanations both lean on a *metaphysical presupposition*, according to which an unobservable entity (God, mental unconscious)—presumably never confirmed to exist—gives rise to the phenomenon. A believer may present additional phenomena in favour of the existence of God, and a Freudian can also talk about, for example, "psychic continuity" (see Talvitie, 2009, pp. 66–67). "Additional evidence" nevertheless does not change the picture, since evidence has a different role in empirical and metaphysical issues.

In empirical claims of the form "A affects (or is a partical cause of) B" it is possible to present evidence that supports or contradicts the claim. The arguments "low level of serotonin causes depression since many depressive people's levels of serotonin are low" and "the unobservable mental unconscious/God exists, since there are such phenomena as psychic disorders, dreams, and hypnotic states" are nevertheless different. In the first place, *phenomena does not prove anything*, but researchers *create theories in order to explain them*. Thus, one should first ask, "How should we explain these phenomena (dreams, psychic disorders, etc.)?", and then perhaps argue that the Freudian (or the religious) explanation is the best one.

The unconscious and "unobservables"

Occasionally—I cannot give references, but I have heard or read this story several times—psychoanalytic folks advocate the idea of the mental unconscious as follows: "The presupposition of the mental unconscious does not violate the principles of science since even in physics it is talked about entities that cannot be observed. When the existence of the unconscious is stubbornly neglected despite the clinical evidence provided by psychoanalytic practice, we deal with a stagnation to the positivistic attitudes prevalent in the beginning of the last century." The story continues with the consideration of whether the terms "psychical" and "mental" should be restricted to consciousness. After hard-to-follow conceptual acrobatics a negative answer is given.

The unconscious is supposed to contain desires, and thus one has to consider it intentional. However, by definition, intentionality is the hallmark of consciousness in particular. This problem carries an advocate of psychoanalytic metaphysics even deeper into frustrating conceptual acrobatics. The outcome is that we cannot rule out the possibility that mental unconscious exists, and psychoanalysis should be taken as a scientific discipline. This logic is worth studying more closely (the supposed intentionality of the unconscious is nevertheless not treated, since I studied it in *The Freudian Unconscious and Cognitive Neuroscience* (Talvitie, 2009, pp. 62–67)).

As mentioned, postivists tried to avoid metaphysical speculation by arguing that knowledge can be based only on observations. The debate between the philosophers Rudolf Carnap and Willard van Orman Quine was the most important single reason that turned philosophers to admit that observation is always more or less theory-laden. That led the scientific community to see the relation between data and theories as more complicated than positivism presumed—observations and theories affect one another in a circulatory manner (see, for example, Chalmers, 1999; Godfrey-Smith, 2003). On this basis, an advocate of psychoanalytic metaphysics might claim that the unconscious is a so-called *unobservable,* which can be "seen" only through psychoanalytic theory.

"Unobservable" is a physicists' and philosophers' term, rarely used in the domains of humanites and neuroscience. In order to illustrate its use, let us take a citation from Carnap:

> Philosophers and scientists have quite different ways of using the terms "observable" and "unobservable". To a philosopher, "observable" has a very narrow meaning. It applies to such properties as "blue", "hard", "hot". These are properties directly perceived by senses .... A philosopher woul not consider a temperature of, perhaps, 80 degrees centigrade, or a weight of 93 1/2 pounds, an observable because there is no direct sensory perception of such magnitudes.
>
> (Carnap, 1995, p. 225)

This does not help us at all in order to treat the unconscious as an unobservable—it seems that as far as the unconscious is an unobservable, it is not the philosophers' one, and actually it is difficult to see what might be the connection between the denial of the unconscious and positivism.

In the history of science there are many examples of how scientists have debated the existence of substances or entities. Debates end either through the giving up of the presupposition of the unobservable in question, or accepting it as reasonable. The latter may mean either that the entity is revealed through a new method of study, or that researchers claim that the current indirect evidence supports the presuppositon.

From the physicists' study of atomic particles we find examples on both of these, and aether and phlogiston are commonly used as examples of presuppositions that were later abandoned. "Aether" refers to a space-filling substance that was presumed to exist by alchemists, natural philosophers, and physicists (early Alfred Einstein among them) until the beginning of the twentieth century. Phlogiston theory, for its part, states that all flammable materials contain phlogiston, which is released during combustion. The theory was developed in the seventeenth century and was still commonly accepted in the middle of the eighteenth. Leicester's (1956, p. 123) statement "Since phlogiston was an elementary principle, its nature could be known only from its effects" sounds familiar to those acquainted with the arguments presented in favour of psychoanalytic metaphysics.

Post-Freudian definitions of the unconscious

In "The unconscious" from the year 1915 Sigmund Freud states: "Indeed, we are obliged to say of some of these latent [unconscious, mental] states that the only respect in which they differ from conscious ones is precisely in the absence of consciousness" (Freud, 1915, p. 168). Freud's statement resembles the paradoxes presented by Zen masters—*What might be the outcome if consciousness were taken away from a conscious state?* Perhaps something similar as when roundness is taken away from a circle, or wetness from water. The following citations reflect psychoanalytic views circa a century later from Freud's original formulations.

Quite astonishingly, Gomez (2005, pp. 9–10) states that (unconscious) psychic reality and the psychical "has no language of its own. It cannot be broken down into mental and physical components, yet it can only be thought of as though it were mental, or as though it were physical." This kind of conceptual acrobatics makes it very hard to form an idea of what mental unconscious is supposed to be. Mental and physical—or rather mental and neurophysical—vocabularies are evidently the (only) alternatives for talking about the unconscious. In the study of consciousness, neurophysiology does not provide evidence for the existence of phenomenal consciousness, and thus the only proof becomes from "the first person point-of-view", that is, through our experiences. By definition, the existence of the mental unconscious will never be proved to exist that way. Since the unconscious does not appear to our consciousness, and is neither a neurophysiological entity, it is difficult to avoid the conclusion that there is no logical possibility on how it might exist.

It is not clear whether Cordelia Schmidt-Hellerau considers the mental unconscious as a construct:

> We more or less take it for granted that an entity such as "the id" has only a theoretical, and not a concrete or real, existence; but even such a basic term as "the unconscious" can be defined in different ways ... the unconscious (as a phenomenon) can be experienced, but not *the system Ucs.*, which is a component of our metapsychological constructions.
>
> (Schmidt-Hellerau, 1995, p. 41; emphasis in original)

Schmidt-Hellerau's stand leaves us wondering how do those analysts not accepting metapsychology—actually the majority of analysts—approach the existence of the mental unconscious.

Gunnar Karlsson's view is not far from Schmidt-Hellerau's:

> I would claim that the unconscious in this most radical form signifies a state that is beyond experience, but nevertheless "inside" the subject. It is something that has never been lived through, something that has never been grasped in conscious experience. The unconscious in its most radical meaning, is not—and has never been—available within the content given in our conscious experiencing .... In other words, the unconscious can only be captured by means of a theoretical construction.
>
> (Karlsson, 2010, p. 79)

M. Guy Thompson, a distinguished psychoanalytic scholar, concludes his essay "The role of being and experience in Freud's unconscious ontology" by stating: "From Heidegger's ontological perspective, the unconscious is not a theoretical construct, nor is it 'in' my head, but 'out' *there*, in the world, a dimension of Being" (Thompson, 2004, p. 26; emphasis in original).

Mark Solms, the leading neuropsychoanalyst, claims that the brain does not cause conscious states, but the unconscious—that he considers as the Kantian *das Ding an sich*—becomes reflected to both conscious and neural processes (Solms, 1997). Thus, the mental unconscious (or mental apparatus) is beyond both consciousness and the brain. As Solms explicitly states, his view strongly contradicts that of both most psychoanalysts and present-day neuroscientists (Talvitie & Ihanus, 2011b).

Perhaps early Freud, the author of "Project", had a fantasy that findings of neuroscience might reveal the mystery of the unconscious. When later Father Freud stressed the mental essence of the unconscious, that emphasis set, in a certain sense, a limit for neuroscience. If neuroscientists would find from the brain something that fitted with Freud's ideas concerning the unconscious (which perhaps they have already done), the psychoanalytic community would not accept it since it would mean that the unconscious is not mental. Thus, the state of things seems to be that we know even beforehand that *the presupposition concerning the mental unconscious will never be proved right or wrong.*

From the scope of psychoanalytic thinking cannot be found a definition for the unconscious that were more informative than the above ones and shared by the majority of psychoanalysts. Considering that we are treating the core idea of the discipline, the divergence of the definitions of the unconsicous is extremely astonishing. What should an outsider think of a discipline that is not able to be more explicit with its object of study? Should we blame him/her for not considering the discipline as scientific? Is it possible for him/her to make a difference between psychoanalysis and the pseudosciences (and religious doctrines)? I think that a negative answer has to be given to both of the last two questions.

Basing on the above considerations and those presented in the second chapter on the mereological fallacy behind the structural model, we might say that for the psychoanalytic community, mental unconscious is like a Rorschach card or a black box (of behaviourism): one can project into it rather freely different kinds of characteristics (desires, fantasies, feelings, and agents), giving it a sort of reality of its own. Psychoanalysis has been very unwilling to "open the box", that is, to describe in a non-metaphorical way what the unconscious is actually supposed to be like and contain. Considering this state of things it is not a surprise that the psychoanalytic idea of the unconscious has been criticised heavily outside the psychoanalytic field (for example, MacIntyre, 1958; O'Brien & Jureidini, 2002; Searle, 1992;

Uleman, 2005, p. 5). As far as I know, Arnold Modell (2003) is the only analyst who has explicitelly resigned the metaphysics behind the unconscious.

The unconscious, the brain, and neuropsychoanalysis

According to psychoanalytic mentalism, the mental unconscious possesses causal power: not just neurophysiological and phenomenal matters, but also repressed memories, ideas, desires, fears, and fantasies are able to cause mental and behavioural acts. The proceeding pages have made it clear that the position of both the materialists and the ordinary mentalists contains certain problems. The psychoanalytic mentalism creates additional problems as well as experiencing those encountered in ordinary mentalism.

Above I treated the existence of the unconscious, and below I willl focus on the *causal relations between the brain, the unconscious, behaviour, and phenomenal states.* Due to the development of neurobiology and the methods of neuroscience, both lay people and researchers are currently very interested in a neuro-viewpoint towards psychological issues. This interest has spread in the domain of psychoanalysis in the form of neuropsychoanalysis. In "On neuropsychoanalytic metaphysics" (Talvitie & Ihanus, 2011b) having been published in *The International Journal of Psychoanalysis*, we introduced with Juhani Ihanus the problems that psychoanalytic mentalism poses for the collaboration with neuroscience. We sketched the following four conceptions, or logical possibilities, through which it is possible to approach the relationships between the unconscious, the brain, and phenomenal states, and behaviour.

In order to form a clear idea of the problem, it is useful to keep in mind a concrete example—consider, for example, Little Hans' fearful reactions when seeing a horse, or a person having a social phobia. In this kind of case, people often have both physical reactions (a trembling of the hands, for example) and phenomenal matters such as anxiety and fantasies concerning what is going to happen in the domain of consciousness. A psychoanalytic mentalist holds that these matters are caused by the mental unconscious. We have to ask how the supposed causal power of the unconscious is related to that of the brain.

For the first, we can think that the activities of the unconscious and the brain take place in a serial manner. Thus, in terms of *the serial conception* either the impulses of the unconscious "go through the brain", or the activities of the unconscious take place after the ones of the brain. The former alternative would mean that—as neuroscientists hold—the brain gives rise to the disorders, but the unconscious triggers those neural processes. In other words, the activity of the unconscious takes place before the activities of the brain. This implies that there are neural processes that possess no neurophysiological cause or "starting point" (and neither have a counterpart in one's experiences and perceptions). This is an astonishing empirical claim, and neuroscientists would not accept that neurons might fire without a reason.

There is also another problem: if the activities of the unconscious take place before those of the brain, how does the unconscious "know", for example, that the person is in a threating situation. Perceptions become formed when physical stimuli become transformed to neural activity, and if unconscious activities preceded neural activity, perceptions would not be available for it. Thus, the unconscious lacked preconditions for proper functioning—Hans' unconscious would not know that there is a horse nearby.

Thus, we should think that if the unconscious and the brain operate in sequence, it is neurophysiological activity that takes place first—neural impulses somehow "go through" the unconscious. This means that in normal situations the unconscious does not make a difference for experiences and behaviour, and a person behaves as would be expected basing on the neural activity. When an intrapsychic conflict is active or relevant in the situation at hand, however, the unconscious causes psychic disorders and slips, distorts perceptions, and so on. In such a case, a person's experiences and reactions are different from what could be expected from the neural activity.

This meant that a non-(neuro)physical matter makes a difference to neurophysical processes—the activity of the brain implies that one were calm, or produced the sentence, "Hereby I open this seminar", but the person's hands tremble (without neurophysical cause), or his lips, tongue, and vocal chords produce the sentence, "Hereby I *close* this seminar". In other words, based on the activity of the brain a person should react and behave in a certain manner, but the unconscious steps in and makes one feel and act differently—again, there is mental or motor activity without neurophysical cause. This is an empirical issue, and neuroscientists do not accept either this version of serialism without convincing evidence. And the burden of proof is on the side of psychoanalytic mentalists.

Parallelism is one possibility for the relation between the unconscious and the brain—the brain and the unconscious operate in parallel, and there is no interaction between them. This *parallel conception* would mean that the unconscious (somehow) gives rise to disorders "directly", separately from the brain. It is difficult to see the concrete difference between the serial and the parallel conceptions. Namely, both conceptions imply that in a "normal situation" the unconscious is causally inert, that is, it does not affect phenomenal states and behaviour. However, when there are intrapsychic conflicts, the unconscious is supposed to be able to cause disorders and other things in an unspecified manner that completely overlooks neurophysiological structures and processes.

Perhaps most psychoanalytic folks are satisfied with both serial and parallel conceptions. Outsiders—especially philosophers and neuroscientists—however, cannot tolerate the above implications of the psychoanalytic mentalism.

When the essence of the mind is studied in the domain of philosophy of the mind, it has been studied whether the (conscious) mind could be seen as an epiphenomenon. In this spirit, we can sketch the *epiphenomenalist conception*. This would mean that psychoanalytic mentalism presumes that the unconscious exists as it has been used to thought in the domain of psychoanalysis, but it does not affect *in itself* to our behaviour and experiences.

The epiphenomenalist conception gives rise to the crucial question of whether or not the unconscious possesses neural correlates. Serial and parallel conceptions presume that the brain and the unconscious are detached systems, and thus the unconscious is not represented at all by the brain. However, similarly as phenomenal matters and contents of consciousness possess neural correlates, there might be neural correlates also for the contents and processes of the mental unconscious.

Such a claim gives rise to an empirical issue of *how we might know that certain neural structure or activity were a correlate of the mental unconscious*. The brain contains 10^{17} cells, and for the most part we cannot explain the activity of them. Thus, there is lot of room for the unconscious correlate-presupposition. However, our unability to explain the activities of the brain in detail is thought to follow from the complexity of it, and it is difficult to ground the argument that certain neural activity reflected the activity of the mental unconscious.

The epiphenomenalist conception means, first, that the unconscious does *not* possess causal power, and second, that the unconscious is actually just an aspect of the brain (similar to the argument that the conscious mind is an aspect of the processes taking place in the brain). From the interdisciplinary viewpoint, the epiphenomenalist conception has a strength: in terms of it the psychoanalytic presupposition of the unconsicous would perhaps be tolerable for outsiders, since it does not imply gaps in neural processess. However, one might ask why one should presume the existence of the mental unconscious if it does not make a difference to our behaviour and experiences. The above considerations on the serial, parallel and epiphenomenalist conceptions seem to lead to an interesting conclusion: if one presumes that there are neural correlates for the unconscious, he or she should also think that the unconscious is causally inert.

Mark Solms, the leading neuropsychoanalyst, has presented a picture on the relations between the brain, the unconscious, and phenomenal states and behaviour that we (Talvitie & Ihanus, 2011b) babtised as the *"Kantian" conception*. Solms (1997) argues that Freudian thinking is anchored to the Kantian idea that beyond both neurophysical processes and phenomenal states lies *das Ding an sich*. Thus, the neural activities of the brain does not cause phenomenal states nor the other way round, but *das Ding an sich* causes both of them. This claim—Solms may well be right that it represent Freud's thinking—is astonishing, and very difficult to accept. It is commonly thought that for example, drugs make a difference to our phenomenal states and behaviour because they affect the brain, but an advocate of the Kantian conception tells a wholly different story. Solms is aware that even his fellow-psychoanalysts do not accept the Kantian conception:

> If I am correct in my suspicion that most psychoanalysts accept that assumption [that conscious experiences are caused by neurophysiological processes], then you will perhaps be surprised to learn that I reject it. It is, I believe a statement to which no psychoanalyst should ever assent, as it flatly contradicts the fundamental assumption on which the whole of our discipline rests. I am aware that in saying this I am implying that our discipline is very much out of step with contemporary research.
>
> (Solms, 1997, pp. 681–682)

The Kantian conception leans on very heavy and difficult metaphysical presuppositions, and we must ask whether a real collaboration is possible between a Kantian neuropsychoanalyst and a non-Kantian neuroscientist. Not surprisingly, the psychoanalytic community has been very critical towards Solms' view (for references, see Talvitie & Ihanus, 2011b). Linda Brakel, for example, states: "I fear, however, that if psychoanalysts embrace Solms's view, with its implication that we need not worry about the dissynchrony between psychoanalysis and the findings and methods of current cognitive/neuroscientific research, our discipline will never be enriched by, or contribute to, explorations of the relationship between mind and brain" (Brakel, 1997, p. 720).

All in all, it is appropriate to conclude that all four conceptions on the relationships between the brain, the unconscious, phenomenal states, and behaviour are very problematic.

Evaluating the presupposition of mental unconscious as a scientfic hypothesis

Neither Freud nor his followers have pinpointed the mental unconscious, and psychoanalysis has not even been able to present an understandable and commonly shared description on the nature of its existence. There is no doubt that the mental unconscious is a metaphysical postulate.

Religions and esoteric movements are based on metaphysical presuppositions concerning different kinds of supernatural forces, entities, and levels of existence. Also in the domain of science, suppositions are made on the existence of unobservables. In order to maintain the demarcation between science and non-science (or pseudo-science), it has to be sketched some kind of rules as to the grounds on which it is legitimate to postulate unobservables—it is not possible to maintain the demarcation if disciplines could postulate non-observables as they wish. The scientific status of the psychoanalytic postulate of the unconscious has to be evaluated on this basis.

William Wimsatt describes the view he develops in the book *Re-engineering Philosophy for Limited Beings: Piecewise Approximations to Reality* as "... a softer, richer vision of our world and our place in it than promised by both sides in the history of the warfare between mentalisms and materialisms. It is a more appropriate philosophy of science, I argued, than we have been given so far" (Wimsatt, 2007, p. ix). His criterion for "regarding something as real or trusthworthy" (Wimsatt, 2001, p. 195) is robustness: "*Things are robust if they are accessible (detectable, measurable, derivable, producible, or the like) in a variety of independent ways*" (Wimsatt, 2007, p. 196; emphasis in original).

On this basis, we can say that the claim "unconscious factors have a significant affect on our behaviour and experiences" is extremely robust: currently it is difficult to find a tradition of research that would deny it. With the presupposition of the mental unconscious, the situation is radically different: it is based solely on a single theoretical tradition (psychoanalysis).

Let us study three criteria in order to evaluate scientific models or theories. First (and evidently), how comprehensive and detailed explanations it can present. Second, which kind of metaphysical presuppositions it leans on. According to the principle called "Occam's razor", we should avoid unnecessary metaphysical presuppositions and favour a theory that is able to explain the phenomena with less metaphysics preuppositions. Third, how a theory fits with existing theories and findings. The evolutionary theory is an example of how a theory can succeed with the last criterion: it is supported by theories and findings from several fields, from different branches of biology to medicine and paleontology.

We must ask: *What actually can be won by making the metaphysical postulate concerning the mental unconscious?* When telling, for example, that a repressed unconscious content (of the mental unconscious) causes a disorder or certain aspects of a dream, it is not clear if anything has really been explained—as far as one cannot give even a preliminary description of the entity that is supposed to cause the phenomenon under scrutiny, it is questionable if we can talk about explanation. The postulate does not seem to solve any problem, but creates one: psychoanalytic mentalism shares all the problems of ordinary mentalism, but, in addition, it fits very badly to the views of present-day neuroscience.

In rather rare cases, a theory is a success although it challenges the presuppositions of the other theories of the field. In Kuhnian terms, this kind of situation is a "paradigm shift": a new theory contains undisputed merits, and the field becomes reorganised around it. However, it is difficult to conceive that Freud's ideas concerning the mental unconscious and consciousness, having been developed a century ago, would give rise to such a paradigm shift.

Theories—and especially wide-ranging theories like that of Freud's—consist of many pieces, and a scientist faces considerable challenges when trying to make them fit together. Thus, metaphysical assumptions concerning the mental unconscious are not a detached part of Freud's theories. Quite contrary: below we will see how Freud's views on the essence of self-reflection (or consciousness) are dependent on his views concerning the mental unconscious.

On the essence of (self-)consciousness

The story about Freud's career as a scientist use to be narrated with a focus to the unconscious. However, we might tell the story from the point of view of self-consciousness as well: Freud was interested in enlargening man's self-consciosness, and tested several methods. At first he used suggestion, later he kept his hand near a patient's head in order to promote concentration, and at last he developed the technique we currently know as the psychoanalytic method.

Freud noted that his patients began to produce memories they seemed not to have had previously, and their slips and dreams referred to desires and fears that they would deny possessing, but that altogether seemed to make some kind of sense from the point of view of their disorders. This notion can be seen as the starting point of his theorising, although the observations, the method of cure, and the theories actually developed in a circular manner.

Since the presupposition of the mental unconscious is one of Freud's "cornerstones", it determines the other parts of the system—his views on the nature of consciousness or self-reflection, among others, are tailored to fit with his view on the unconscious. When it comes to consciousness, Freud's solution was to argue that it is like an organ of perception: "In psycho-analysis there is no choice for us but to assert that mental processes are in themselves unconscious, and to liken the perception of them by means of consciousness to the perception of the external world by means of the sense organs" (Freud, 1915, p. 171; see Solms, 1997). Did he had alternatives? As far as memories and desires emerging in the course of the cure are thought to have pre-existed in the unconscious mind, consciousness has to be seen as a faculty that "perceives" the contents when defences relax. Actually, a century ago there was nothing extraordinary in Freud's view, and, for example, William James and Wilhelm Wundt approached self-consciousness in a rather "Freudian" manner (Valentine, 1992, p. 54).

Let us stress—again—that Freud's analogy between perceiving and (self-)consciousness is a metaphor. Sense organs are neural systems, but consciousness, if anything, is mental. Each sense organ reacts to certain specific kinds of physical stimuli, but what are the stimuli that consciousness receives? We may perceive objects that exist in the outer world, but what is actually the world and the objects that consciousness perceives? These questions are hard to answer. It is difficult to avoid the impression that Freud's view on the nature of (self-)consciousness would have been different if he had not the doctrine about unconscious mental life to defend.

In the previous chapters we have found that both psychological terms in general, and *conscious* desires, fears, and beliefs presumed by folk-psychology, should be seen as constructs. It is very difficult to make fit into that picture the idea that self-reflection were perceptions of mental objects. Actually, there is a vast body of empirical evidence that introspective statements are rather theory-laden constructs prone to errors than (neutral) reports on perceptions (see, for example, Bargh, 2005; Nisbett & Ross, 1980). In general, the idea that we have inner states that could be observed, and that we might have direct access to the causes of our acts, appears in the light of present-day views (for example, Audi, 1998, pp. 77–80; Dretske, 1997, pp. 39–63; Smith, 2010; Stalnaker, 2008) simply as odd and erroneous.

One might ask: "But we surely possess feelings, ideas, and so on, and it is clear that at some moments we know them rather well, and at other moments very badly. If it is really such a bad idea that we may or may not perceive such mental matters, how should we explain the enlargening of one's self-knowledge or the fruits of introspection?" Determining the nature of self-knowledge in an exact manner is a tricky task, and there are many possibilities to, for example, fill the sentence "Peter___that he is angry". In everyday talk we can say at least that Peter *notices, recognises, realises,* or *becomes aware* of that matter. But what actually is that mental act in essence? In the next chapter I will approach this issue. My main point will be that self-consciousness or self-reflection is entangled to language in a much more complex way than the psychoanalytic tradition has recognised.

Psychoanalytic metaphysics—a voluntary straitjacket?

All in all, the metaphysics behind psychoanalytic mentalism is very confusing, and we might say that in terms of metaphysical postulates psychoanalysis is in the margins of science for good reasons. It seems that here Freudian thinking possesses a complex set of problems. In order to explain his clinical findings, Freud made the problematic metaphysical presupposition of the mental unconscious. That presupposition tied his hands concerning the essence of consciousness. It was very beneficial for the scientific credibility of psychoanalysis to abandon nineteenth-century metaphysics. The core idea of *The Freudian Unconscious and Cognitive Neuroscience* (Talvitie, 2009) was to show how this can be done—how psychoanalytic ideas concerning the unconscious can be based on the ordinary mentalism and current views of cognitive neuroscience.

These reflections (and claims) give rise to a question: Why does psychoanalysis still lean, despite its evident problems, on hundred-year-old metaphysical doctrines, refusing to develop better ones or replace them with the current ideas of behavioural sciences, and that way marginalise itself as a discipline? Why does psychoanalysis paint itself in the corner this way, and is even proud of that?

For the later Father Freud, the mental essence of the unconscious was a dogma that psychoanalysis should never abandon. He stated:

> The assumption that there are unconscious mental processes, the recognition of the theory of resistance and repression, the appreciation of the importance of sexuality and of the Oedipus complex—these constitute the principal subject-matter of psycho-analysis and the foundations of its theory. No one who cannot accept them all should count himself a psycho-analyst.
>
> (Freud, 1923a, p. 247)

Freud formed a secret committee (the members even had rings) in order to defend these dogmas after his death (Grosskurth, 1991). In his study about the dynamics of psychoanalytic institutions, Reeder (2004, pp. 59–114) suggests that the foundational aim of analytic training is to convey the candidates a conviction for the existence of the unconscious (see also Davies, 2009).

On this basis, it is not surprising at all that in psychoanalytic circles the existence of the unconscious is normally taken for granted, and there is a lack of sincere interest in studying whether the postulate is plausible. A similar spirit can characterise apologies of (the scientific standing of) psychoanalysis: a critical reader easily remains suspicious as to whether the author is genuinely interested in the demarcation problem and the characteristics of science.

The mental unconscious constitutes psychoanalyts' and psychodynamic therapists' clinical work as a study of the deepest mysteries of the human mind. Such an idea of one's profession is probably also significant for a psychoanalyst's and a psychodynamic therapist's identity: without the mental unconscious, psychodynamists were just ordinary clinicians, not very different from other psychotherapists.

CHAPTER SIX

Narration, the Wittgensteinian revolution(s), and becoming conscious of the repressed—why psychoanalysis is more about the language, and less about the brain

I realised the significance of the viewpoint of narration one summer in the mid-1990s. I had read all Milan Kundera's novels, and a vague idea emerged in my mind: stories self-evidently consist of different kinds of events, incidents, and affairs taking place in the physical and social worlds and in fictive people's minds, but they seem to have another aspect, too. I had a presentiment that Kundera has (or follows) some kind of *system* in his narration. When meeting one of my friends, a poet who studied literature at university, I asked him what might be the discipline or branch of study analysing that aspect of stories. He answered straight off: "Yeah, that's narratology. Classical works are Wayne Booth's *The Rhetoric of Fiction* and Seymour Chatman's *Story and Discourse: Narrative Structure in Fiction and Film.*"

I bought those classics and learnt that stories may be told by an author, or one or several characters of the story. I also made the notion that it makes a considerable difference as to whether a story is told in chronological order or otherwise—one cannot start a detective story by telling who committed the murder (probably most people need not read the classics of narratology in order to comprehend this matter). Booth's (1961) and Chatman's (1978) works contained also the idea that we should think that stories may contain both implicit and explicit authors and readers.

Narratology inspired me a lot, and I realised that psychoanalysis may be studied from that perspective, too. I was not the first to think (see, for example, Loewenstein, 1992) that in case studies a psychoanalyst often appears as a character resembling Sherlock Holmes, and that narration in them is often similar to that of detective stories: what was behind the mystery is revealed in the end. I also made a kind of "narrative experiment". In "hard-boiled" detective stories it is often described meetings of the detective and clients, and encounters between psychiatrists and psychotherapists and their clients are not wholly different from them. Thus, I mixed the styles between hard-boiled detective stories and psychotherapists' case studies: I wrote a short novel about the meeting of a (male) psychiatrist and a (beautiful female) client, where the style was a (more or less artistic) pastiche on Raymond Chandler's detective stories.

In the first half of the twentieth century the narrative approach had not yet emerged, and thus it is clear that Freud and his collaborators were rather insensitive concerning the role of language. "Making the repressed conscious", the aim of the psychoanalytic talking-cure, was sketched (on a theoretical level) rather mechanically as just adding word-representations to thing-representations. In the second half of the twentieth century, the viewpoint of language and narration became actually rather popular in the domain of psychoanalysis: Jacques Lacan held that his linguistic view reflected the true nature of Freud's thinking; Paul Ricoeur laid grounds for the hermeneutic conception of psychoanalysis; Julia Kristeva, Jacques Derrida, and others mixed psychoanalytic viewpoints to the philosophy of language; narrative psychoanalysis emerged.

In the current era of rapidly developing brain-research, psychoanalysis appears to many people in the spirit of Freud's "Project" as a proto-natural science. It is thought that psychoanalysis might get a full membership among natural sciences if it would go more into neuroscience. For me such a view appears as neglecting the humanistic side of psychoanalysis. In order to underline the limits of the neuroscience-oriented conception of psychoanalysis, below I will create a viewpoint to psychoanalytic issues that stresses the role of language as strongly as I feel reasonable. In order to avoid exhausting formal considerations of this philosophical topic, I will treat the subject matter in a (relatively) free manner.

The Wittgensteinian revolution(s) and psychoanalysis

How do psychological concepts such as "desire", "envy", and "shame" relate to the states of mind that they are supposed to refer to? For the first generation of psychoanalysts the relation was unproblematic: for statements like "Hans fears [consciously or unconsciously] X" or "Anna desires [consciously or unconsciously] Y" there are simply corresponding states of mind. As far as I know, Freud and his collaborators were not aware that their thinking is very close to the view that another Viennese-born genius, Ludwig Wittgenstein, advocated in his early masterpiece *Tractatus Logico-Philosophicus* (Wittgenstein, 1922).

Wittgenstein was able to create two times a fresh new perspective on the world, and he was responsible for bringing language to the centre of philosophy. Thus, it is not surprising that he is commonly held as the most significant philosopher of the twentieth century. He made also specific remarks on psychoanalysis (see Bouveresse, 1996). However, here it is more important to create a general image of the place of psychoanalysis in the post-Wittgenstein world, than study those remarks in detail.

In his later works, Wittgenstein (especially Wittgenstein, 1953) argued against his earlier Tractatus-view and suggested that we always approach phenomena from a certain viewpoint using certain terminology ("language game"), and that there is no "objective" way to describe anything. Although not referring to Wittgenstein, Charles Taylor (1985) makes a Wittgensteinian distinction on two views on the nature of language. He characterises the former (Tractatus-) view by stating that language is seen as an instrument, and that "discovering the meaning of words is finding what ideas or things they stood for" (Taylor, 1985, p. 9). Whilst the former view focuses on words, sentences are crucial for the latter (late-Wittgenstein) view. Taylor states that in terms of the latter view: "Certain ways of being, of feeling, of relating to each other are only possible given certain linguistic resources," and adds that "language not only depicts, but also articulates and makes things manifest, and in so doing helps shape our form of life" (Taylor, 1985, p. 10). We might say that in terms of the Freudian Tractatus-view language (objectively) *describes* the world, whereas the view created by late Wittgenstein presumes that with the help of language we *create* worlds.

Wittenstein is known as an obscure, partly mystical, philosopher. His later works gave rise to different kinds of relativism and narrative approaches. Even the critics of these approaches have to admit that in the post-Wittgensteinian era the question concerning the relations between distinct scientific paradigms is very complicated.

According to late Wittgenstein, all perceptions, theories, and explanations are tied to ones's interests, presuppositions, vocabulary, and perspective. This basic view contains radical consequences. It makes it impossible to see the relations between scientific disciplines as hierarchically ordered (natural sciences forming a solid bottom, into which humanistic theories might be reduced), and even the idea of objective knowledge becomes questionable. I will not go deeper into the waters of the philosophy of science. For us, the crucial thing is that late Wittgenstein questioned the idea that a word or a theory might describe a state of things of the world in a neutral and objective manner.

In the case of certain concepts it is possible to pinpoint the objects the concept refers to. As the first chapters made evident, psychological terms are not among them: they are constructs that may refer at the same time to mental states, acts, behavioural dispositions, and personal characteristics. When approaching them from the perspective of folk-psychology, we note that psychological concepts such as "anger", "joy", and "pain" are taught to us as children—"Uuh, you are surely angry since Tim took your toy"; "You seem to be happy seeing father again"; "Ah, hitting a toe that way surely hurts!" As members of the linguistic community we learn to use psychological and other concepts in an appropriate way, and in a foundational sense we have no alternative ("private languge") for that. Taylor states that in order to understand the concepts of folk-psychology "we have to be in on a certain experience, we have to understand a certain language, not just words, but also a certain language of mutual action and communication, by which we blame, exhort, admire, esteem each other. In the end we are in on this because we grow up in the ambit of certain common meanings" (Taylor, 1985, p. 24).

When Freud laid the grounds of psychoanalysis, the scientific world both contained reflections from romanticism and faced the challenge/promise of positivism, and language was seen as as an innocent mediator of scientific ideas. Thus, Freud's theories went in terms of nearly concrete entities (like conscious/unconscious desire/fantasy, ego, psychic tension, and instinctual energy) which become transformed and are related to one another through definable processes (repression, intellectualisation, sublimation, secondary process). Freudian and also non-Freudian psychoanalytic theories yield Freud's romantic-positivistic worldview, and as far as this state of things is not fully recognised, it is not possible to have reasonable discussions on the scientific status of psychoanalysis. *In the post-Tractatus world the above mentioned psychoanalytic terms, among others, should be seen as constructs.*

Below I will bring the above philosopical issues into the clinical reality of psychotherapy by sketching how repression and becoming conscious of the repressed should be seen in the post-Wittgensteinian frames of thinking. Considering the conclusion of the previous chapter, it is not a surpise that the core issue is to avoid Freud's metaphysical commitments concerning the unconscious and (self-) consciousness.

Enlargening of self-consciousness as a process of construction

According to present-day views, memories are not coded in the brain and retrieved from there. Instead, remembering is held to be a constructive process, in which (fragmentary and partial) memory-traces only provide a basis for cognitive processes, which lead to the experience of remembering the previous event. In these terms, repression of a memory means that the *construction of the previous event into the domain of consciousness is inhibited or distorted.* As argued in the previous chapters, none of our conscious beliefs, desires, and knowlege exist as such in our minds and brains—they, too, become formed in our consciousness through cognitive processess, and thus repression of them has to be seen in terms of inhibition or distortion of those processes. This kind of emphasis on processes is the foundation of the view developed below.

As a clinical phenomenon the process of becoming conscious of the repressed is dynamic and lively, but the Freudian theoretical formulation of it appears as mechanical and opaque: the repressed idea is coded in the unconscious (let us note that we do not know how, since we do not know what the unconscious is like); due to the working-through having taken place in therapy, censorship ceases to repress it (we have no idea how that might be expressed through the current concepts and models of behavioural sciences); a word-representation is added to the idea (again, we do not know how that might be expressed in present-day terms); the representation of the idea becomes transformed from the domain of primary-process to that of secondary-process (an outsider cannot make sense of the talk about these two different processes); and due to the above matters, consciousness is able to "perceive" the previously repressed idea (see the criticism presented in the previous chapter on Freud's consciousness-as-perception-metaphor).

For Freud "adding a word-representation" is (on a theoretical level) a simple mechanical act, and—in the spirit of early Wittgenstein's *Tractatus*—the relation between unconscious (as well as conscious) mental content and its verbal description is direct and non-problematic. The lesson of late Wittgenstein was that the relation between words and their references is extremely problematic and complex. Thus, we should think that mental contents, too, are always verbalised from a certain viewpoint, using certain terms that the folk-psychology of one's culture happens to provide.

Psychoanalytic literature typically approaches the interaction between analysts and analysands on an idealised and abstracted level—the interaction is described in a theory-laden way using psychoanalytic concepts. Anssi Peräkylä and his collaborators (Peräkylä, 2005, 2010; Vehviläinen, 2003) have recorded psychoanalytic sessions (as well as interactions in other professional settings) and studied transcriptions of them in terms of conversation analysis. They create towards clinical psychoanalysis a perspective that is not dependent on psychoanalytic terminology, and thus their works make it possible to approach psychoanalytic topics without committing to (any of the) psychoanalytic theories. The psychoanalytic community typically stresses the importance of interdisciplinary studies on "psychoanalytic" topics, and nowadays neuropsychoanalysis seems to possess almost a hegemony to interdisciplinarity. However, we must not overlook this kind of interdisciplinary study having been put forward in the domain of humanities.

When reading the studies of Peräkylä's group, it is difficult to maintain the Freudian romantic-positivistic conception of becoming conscious of the repressed. Transcriptions make explicit how analysts' interpretations are possible only if he or she constructs the matters told by an analysand in a certain way, and takes a certain perspective towards them. Peräkylä's studies explicate the fact (which every clinician and analysand knows) that the clinical process called "becoming conscious of the unconscious" consists of several matters: the analyst directs his or her attention to certain matters in the analysand's narration, and by verbalising his/her notions directs also the analysand's attention to them; the analyst conceptualises those matters in a certain way; the analyst brings apprently distinct matters together with the help of interpretations; the analysand and the analyst elaborate the interpretations together.

When describing the process in such a down-to-earth manner, one may get the impression that in the Freudian story about bringing ideas from the domain of the unconscious into the scope of consciousness, the emperor has no clothes. The insights concerning one's own mental life should not be conceptualised as bringing an idea from one (mental) place to another, but by creating constructions that appear as accurate and therapeutically beneficial. Let us make this idea more accessible by considering becoming conscious of repressed sexual desire and envy basing on the so-called four-level model (see Talvitie, 2009; Talvitie & Tiitinen, 2006).

A's sexual desire towards B has several cognitive and affective components. First, it feels something to have such a desire. However, it is possible not to recognise the feeling, or to misrecognise it as non-sexual excitement. This means that the feeling is not fully distinctive. Second, sexual desire may be accompanied by genital arousal. Directing of attention is critical with both arousal and the feeling of desire—if one does not direct attention to them, they may take place without one noticing. Third, sexual desire has an object. In order to possess a sexual desire, one must at least recognise someone as a possible partner for intercourse, and usually there are also fantasies about that.

According to Freud's romantic-positivistic line of thought the mind contains sexual desires, and one may or may not be conscious of them. However, since sexual desire (as well as other desires) consists of such components, it is not possible that a desire were an enitity that would lie in the unconscious: the unconscious does not contain either feelings or genitals that might become aroused. Since psychoanalysis cannot tell the form of existence of the mental unconscious, it is unclear how the object of desire should be supposed to be represented by it.

Thus, it seems that the same holds with sexual desire as with (most) other psychological concepts: a term does not refer to a single distinctive mental entity; instead, it is a construct, which may possess several behavioural and phenomenal components. "Deconstruction" of the term envy goes as follows.

From the cognitive perspective, the term "envy" means that a) a person wants to possess something, but does not; and b) another person possesses that matter (or at least the envious person thinks so). Although envy does not belong to the lists of basic and advanced emotions created by the researchers of emotion, envy surely possesses an affective component, too—it feels something to be envious. When one is just "mildly" envious, he or she recognises the feeling and knows which matters give rise to it. When being *really* envious, we often present bitter comments to or about the envied person, or deny, downgrade, or undermine his or her achievements. Thus, envy is a typical psychological concept: it is not a mental entity that could be "perceived", but a construct consisting of several components.

In the (theoretical) Freudian frames of thinking the crucial questions concerning the process of becoming conscious of the repressed idea would be: *How and why did consciousness become capable of perceiving envy/sexual desire?* and *How and why did the ego/censorship cease to maintain defences*? My deconstruction of "desire" and "envy" may sound theoretical, too. However, the above analysis can also be seen as simply descriptions on the correct use of those folk-psychological terms. Namely, if an educated person were asked to define "desire" and "envy", he or she would tell those same matters (although probably in a less formal manner).

Let us think of becoming conscious of one's desire or envy in psychotherapy. The client/analysand tells about his feelings and associations concerning the other person in the time period of several hours, weeks, or months. At first he would categorially deny his desire/envy, if the therapist would present such an interpretation. Gradually "the material" evidently implies that it dealt with envy/sexual desire: the client's descriptions concerning the interaction with the other person, his associations of them, the tone or spirit of his speech, refers to sexual desire/envy. Regardless of whether it is actually the therapist or the client themselves that at last presents the interpretation of the material, it can be formulated for our purposes as follows: *In our linguistic community the term "sexual desire"/"envy" is used to describe the complex of feelings, ideas, fantasies, and acts that have emerged during the past hours/weeks/months.*

Thus, an entity desire/envy has not become brought from the unconscious into the domain of consciousness. Instead, the psychoanalytic setting has made the client, first, produce fantasies and associations, attend to his feelings and ideas (the basic rule of psychoanalysis is to tell every idea that comes to one's mind regardless of whether it seems important), and to note connections between apparently distinct matters. Second, he has (reluctantly) accepted that considering the "evidence", the word "desire"/"envy" is the appropriate one to describe his relation to the other person.

I believe that when reflecting the clinical process of how one actually becomes conscious of something, Freudian theoretical concepts and especially the metaphor of consciousness as perception are not especially enlightening. The above process-view, based on the Wittgensteinian conception of psychological concepts and the current views of cognitive neurocience, succeeds much better. When explaining the phenomenon of enlargening self-consciousness/becoming conscious of the repressed, Freud drew the crucial line between the unconscious and consciousness. The above implies that the line should be drawn differently.

When an idea or perception is not attended to, it rapidly vanishes from the domain of consciousness, and is not remembered later. Thus, being conscious of something is not the issue. In terms of the above process-view, the power of the psychoanalytic setting lies rather in making an analysand connect apparently distinct matters (or to recognise patterns of behaviour and experiencing), and "pulling" the states of consciousness into the scope of self-consciousness.

In the ordinary situations of life we typically forget fleeting ideas, feelings, and associations due to the affairs taking place around us—the activities of the outer world enable us to non-attend to the contents of consciousness that are disturbing. Contrary to that, in psychoanalysis one lies on a couch in a state of a certain kind of sensoric deprivation, and that makes it difficult to non-attend to one's feelings and ideas. The basic rule of psychoanalysis makes non-attending even more difficult: When being reluctant to report a certain state of consciousness, one knows at the same time that remaining silent about it would mean "breaking the rule", and that creates a pressure to verbalise it to the therapist. On the other hand, silence would endorse the significance of the idea. These anxious thoughts keep the analysand processing the confusing idea or feeling, and thus it becomes drawn in the domain of self-consciousness even if one in the end does not verbalise it.

Process-thinking makes us note that along with verbalisation a conscious state becomes enriched or elaborated. Creating a satisfactory linguistic form for a state of consciousness demands cognitive processes (thinking), and that process makes the state more sophisticated. When the state is named a certain kind of "fear" or "desire", for example, it does not just become named, but also drawn into a domain of other verbalised mental matters, or web of meanings. Along with verbalisation the state becomes set in the class of other states of a similar kind. That enables the analysand to compare the state to other similar states, and in that way the nature or identity of the state in question becomes clearer. Due to verbalisation, in the future one will also apply to the state the rules of folk-psychology: when saying to possess, for example, a fear, one also implies having a certain kind of feeling, avoiding a certain object (a person or situation) if possible, and so on.

On the psychodynamics of narration

When studying above the intimate relation between language and self-understanding, we have restricted ourselves to the naming of mental states. The relation becomes even more complex when applying the viewpoint of narration, introduced at the beginning of the chapter.

Whatever story can be told in countless orders—chronologically, from the end to the beginning, or using flashbacks. Thus, narrative structure makes a difference in detective stories and novels, as well as in the context of psychotherapy. Consider a client/analysand having done something shameful, for example, having accused someone without reason in a very aggressive manner. When telling about the incident to a therapist, one may begin from the end by stating, "I told Bill very aggressively that he is guilty of Cindy's problems. That is surely not true, and I am very ashamed, guilty, and upset about my behaviour." Such a "straight to the core of things" narrative strategy is common to news reports, for example.

A reverse narrative strategy would be to begin with how Bill invited some people for dinner, continue by telling how everybody drank quite a lot, and to end the tale with how—as everybody knows—in such situations sometimes sad things happen (at least in Finland). It is easy to see how these narrative strategies possess psychodynamic functions.

The latter narrative strategy might be called "detective story" or "Hollywood film structure", which saves the dramatic revelation to the end. Telling about the incident that way presents the client's behaviour as more understandable, and reduces the anxiety felt by him. From the perspective of the relation between the therapist and the client, we can make the notion that when using this kind of narrative strucure, a client intrigues the therapist similarly as the writer of a detective story does with his or her reader.

We must not think that the former strategy were simply a frank one lacking psychodynamic functions. The strategy presents the client as some kind of wrongdoer, and it might be thought to reflect a masochist tendency or a demanding super-ego. The crucial notion (in the spirit of late Wittgenstein) here is that we *cannot determine the concepts and narrative strategy that would make matters appear as they really are.*

Conclusion

In Freud's romantic-positivistic world psychodynamics occur in the psyche, and language is used in order to describe it. In terms of the Wittgensteinian process-view *language is the domain in which psychodynamics take place.* Conscious states come and go, and as far as one is forgotten rapidly, it does not become a problem for the person. Defences and repression may step in when one aims at attending to a conscious state (through which it would become part of self-consciousness) or to verbalise it (through which it would become under the logic of folk-psychology). Thus, repression and defences seem to concern verbalisations: one is reluctant to draw together different matters, and name the outcome as the surrounding folk-psychology necessitates. To put it in other words: repression and defences appear as inhibiting, interrupting, and distorting the process in which one's phenomenal and behavioural matters are verbalised and narrated.

On this basis we can make three general notions. First, since psychological terms are constructs and our self-knowledge is always based on non-scientific folk-psychology based on the surrounding culture, a psychotherapist or psychoanalyst (or anyone else) is not in a position to tell what is a correct verbalisation for a certain phenomenal or behavioural matter. However, a therapist may nevertheless note when a client systematically verbalises his or her phenomenal and behavioural world in a distorted and/or restricted manner, and violates the logic of folk-psychology. We must think that basing his own therapy, training, and position as an outsider observer, a therapist is able to make (only) notions and suggestions ("interpretations") that are on average realist or appropriate. For psychodynamic and other psychotherapy there is no more "objective" basis than this.

Second, the above implies that defences affect our narration in the first place, or that they should be located (at least for the most part) between consciousness and narrative self-consciousness.

Third, when we note that psychotherapy is entangled to language to the extent presented above, the significance of neuroscience for psychoanalysis is more limited than has been typically thought by the advocates of neuropsychoanalysis.

CHAPTER SEVEN

Is it possible to be scientific (enough) outside of the scientific community?

Psychodynamic therapies are roughly as effective as psychotherapies in general (Cooper, 2008; Shedler, 2010). Although classical psychoanalysis is often seen as "treatment", psychodynamic therapies—psychoanalysis as it is applied today among them—belong to the class of psychotherapies that to lesser extent try to "treat" people. In general, humanistic ideals are in many ways embedded deep into the psychoanalytic ethos: it is aimed at supporting clients' autonomy, and psychic problems are relieved through enlargening self-understanding. Due to these humanistic basic attitudes, psychodynamic therapists avoid manipulative techniques, are reluctant to give advice, and take pains to not silently advocate their own values to the clients.

A psychodynamic clinician is also not restricted in their interests to disorders, since he or she is always interested in a client's whole life. Psychoanalytic techniques, or I would rather talk about professionals' ways of working, are genuinely explorative, which means that it is possible to find matters that may have not been searched for. Let us still note that psychoanalysis is not only a psychotherapists' background theory, since it is widely applied outside the clinical context. We might say that psychoanalysis is a tool that enables us to see the world differently.

Considering the above strengths, it should not be possible that psychoanalysis would fade into the margins.

From hickory science to the games of the contemporary academic world

In our times many people are fascinated with different kinds of "retro" things—cars, clothes, guitars, and that like. In golf that trend appears as enthusiasm towards old clothes and hickory clubs. Hickory golf societies are organised into two divisions. Members of the pre-1900 divisions hit old-school Gutta-Percha balls with clubs having been made in the nineteenth century (authorised reproductions being accepted). In the pre-1930 divisions the clubs are slightly younger, and use of modern golf balls is allowed.

When discussing "Freudian matters" with my friend called Emanuel, a psychoanalyst who also plays golf, I occasionally talk about hickory science. I have sworn that I would beat my friend (who usually wins matches against me) by eighteen strokes if he played with hickory clubs. Perhaps the reader guesses the intended moral of my hickory-story: Psychoanalytic concepts and ideas were once fresh and up to date (Kitcher, 1992), but beginning from the 1970s or 1980s psychoanalysis was marginalised. Like those hickory golfers, psychoanalysis has been very interested in its own tradition, and strickingly uninterested in the development taking place around it.

In discussions and writings, psychoanalytic folks rather often tell that a certain researcher's recent finding indicates that a certain idea, notion, or theory of Freud's is true. Behind this kind of thinking there seems to lie a wish that the academic world would return to use those century-old Freudian terms. The idea also seems to imply that one shares early (*Tractatus-*) Wittgenstein's view on the relation between words and the state of things: there are state of things for which a certain Freudian expression is the correct one.

However, it is unconceivable that there were an academic game of our times in which the "Freudian hickory science"—by the expression I refer to hundred-year-old concepts and metaphors not used outside psychoanalysis—might be successful. The others will surely not begin to use again those retro clubs (psychoanalytic concepts), and psychoanalysis will not be given a privilege to maintain an academic reservate (or given a handicap for being old-fashioned).

In the preceding pages the scientific standing of psychoanalysis has been studied from several perspectives. The main problems can be tightened to two issues. First, psychoanalysis' relation to its terminology is … one might use the terms "earnest", "old-fashioned" (in terms of the philosophy of science), and "non-self-conscious". Psychological concepts are typically thought to be constructs, but in psychoanalytic circles most people seem to think that, for example, "ego", "primary process", "Oedipus complex", and "repressed idea" pinpoint "things" or entities in the human. As argued in Chapter Three and Chapter Five, this means that psychoanalytic folks make metaphyscial assumptions not shared by other disciplines.

In the domains of psychotherapy, consulting, and psychiatry there are several disciplines where the interests are close to those of psychoanalysis, and where in the scope there has been made similar observations as psychodynamic therapists. One might think that there is necessarily notable translatability between terminologies, and that each discipline could change to use—at least for a moment—concepts of another discipline.

As far as an advocate of psychoanalysis bases their thinking on psychoanalytic metaphysics and holds that psychoanalytic concepts are not constructs, he or she is forced to think that the change of vocabulary would work only on a very superficial level: only psychoanalytic theories are able to reveal the true causes of clinical phenomena. In practice this kind of thinking implies that psychoanalysis and each of its schools cannot be genuinely open-minded towards other viewpoints.

From the academic point of view it is clear that psychoanalysis cannot withdraw behind its metaphysics in such an arrogant manner. Thus, by (still) holding onto its own terminology and peculiar metaphysics, psychoanalysis actually ensures that it will be in the marginals of the science also in the future. Theoretical—or we might even say "ideological"—principles exceed practical and clinical issues.

The second main problem of psychoanalysis is slightly peculiar: psychoanalytic theoreticians, especially Freud, have had a tendency to "try to explain too much". When taking a look at the fields of psychiatry and psychotherapies, we find that behind disorders there are lots of possible causes; no one is able tell excatly what they are, and they vary depending on the patient (see Chapter Three). When dealing with whatever complex idiosynchratic phenomena—be it psychic disorder, success of a band or play, the weather of a particular place, revolution, or economical depression—it is never possible to present well-founded detailed explanations. In this state of things it is not realistic for any branch of psychiatry or psychotherapy to present anything more than explanatory sketches. Perhaps Freud's heroic ideals have been so suggestive that it has not been recognised that being "scientific enough" is something much more modest than has been typically thought in psychoanalytic circles.

But if psychoanalysis became scientific enough by giving up its metaphysics, turned to keep its terms as constructs, and contented to explain much less than it has been used to doing, would we get anything but a watered-down psychoanalysis? Such a turn might also be thought as sacrificing theoretical shibbolets on the altar of reasonable psychotherapeutic practices. Then the identity of psychoanalytics were determined by describing *the psychoanalytic ethos in a rather practical manner* and telling *what psychodynamic psychotherapists actually do and avoid from doing*.

By sticking to pompous rhetoric, the alternative is a "bold and ominipotent" psychoanalysis, which would rather remain on the margins than listen to lessons on the principles of science. However, even an advocate of this kind of "metaphysical" psychoanalysis has to admit that psychoanalysis has developed around observable clinical and other phenomena.

Psychoanalytic folks believe that there are interesting and significant connections between jokes, values, defences, sexual desires, psychic problems, early experiences, and art, among others. If this kind of matter cannot be shown and described by using terminology that is understandable and acceptable for outsiders, one begins to wonder whether the emperor has clothes. Thus, as far as the findings are not artefacts—and the psychoanalytic community is convinced they are not—psychoanalytic notions, claims, and explanations could be made understandable in the current academic forums.

Scientific community, clinicians' communities, and psychoanalysis

For the most part, discussions concerning the scientific status of psychoanalysis concentrate on the accuracy of psychoanalytic claims, that is, psychoanalytic theories and models. That was also the viewpoint of the previous chapters. However, the scientific status of a discipline can be approached except in terms of its *theories*, also from the perspective of the *scientific community* (entailing also humanistic disciplines), and *procedures of how theories are evaluated*.

What are the characteristics of an organisation or a community that is good at creating well-founded beliefs? The members should be brainy, no doubt, but there should also be shared rules for communication, rules which support the emergence of new ideas and detecting faults from the old ones.

Similar to other people, researchers want to be respected professionals, and so they try to play the game called "science" as well as they can. In that game, the most rewarded matters are creating a well-founded fresh idea, and showing an old, generally accepted idea as erroneous. The more commonly accepted an idea a researcher succeeds in challenging, and the more unlikely an idea he or she is able to show as well-founded, the more successful is the study. Thus, science is characterised by a survival-of-the-fittest logic.

The moral of the above description is that the strengths of science should not be projected to persons, but to the community. Similar to all human activities, science is fallible, and its procedures have weaknesses. As we know, for example, a blind peer-review system does not guarantee objectivity, and occasionally even the most prominent scientists degenerate to defend their own "truths". The principles according to which the scientific community functions nevertheless strongly support the critical evaluation of ideas. What should we think about the capability of psychoanalysis to evaluate critically its own ideas (theories)?

Psychoanalytic journals follow more or less strictly the principles of scientific publishing. However, they have often become formed in the scope of specific school of psychoanalysis, and their more or less explicit goal is to promote founders' views (Stepansky, 2009). As mentioned, from the scientific communities we find the same faults as from other human organisations. However, it may be the case that politics plays a more significant role in psychoanalytic journals than in scientific journals in general.

Consider the essence of introspection, or Freud's view on the nature of consciousness. As presented in the previous chapter, with this topic there is a remarkable tension between psychoanalytic views and prevailing mainstream ones. However, it seems that the psychoanalytic community either is not aware of the tension, or does not care about it: PEP-web (Psychoanalytic Electronic Publishing), a psychoanalytic literature search (www.p-e-p.org), reveals eight articles having the term "introspection" in the title, and none recognises the tension in question. If psychoanalysis were a scientific research-community, it would react immediately to such articles as, for example, Renée Smith's (2010) "Against treating introspection as perception-like". It seems that psychoanalytic journals are lacking dynamics that would lead to theories' survival-of-the-fittest fight.

Communities that have emerged around the schools of psychotherapy are clinicians' communities. They lack many of the functions of scientific communities, and they possess ones that scientific communities do not have—foster the training, public image, and interests of psychotherapists, among others. Thus, one should not blame psychoanalysis for not having been able to maintain self-correctiviness of theories typical for science—a community designed for clinicians' purposes cannot be supposed to do the same things as a scientific community. This matter possesses a practical side, too: psychoanalytic folks are mainly clinicians, and full-time researchers are needed in order to put forward studies meeting the standards of present-day science.

Let us remind ourselves that in Chapter three I argued that we should not think that any psychotherapeutic practice could be scientific. In the domains of psychotherapy and psychiatry, as well as in other practical affairs, it is often not possible to make anything more than just informed guesses on the causes of phenomena. Often professionals have to make decisions although their knowledge on the relevant factors of the phenomenon were severely limited. Thus, a practical affair such as psychotherapy can be scientific primarily by leaning on the scientific study on the issues relevant for the activity in question. On this basis we should not ask psychoanalysis and other schools of psychotherapies for more than being scientific *enough*.

Anyway, psychoanalysis cannot be scientific enough by its own, and as Freud as well as present-day psychoanalytic authors (see, for example, Kernberg, 2011; Sonnenberg, 2011; Wallerstein, 2011) think, psychoanalysis should aim at getting a strong foothold in the academic world.

Above I have been arguing that the scientific standing of disciplines can be evaluated from three perspectives: the scientific credibility of theories; procedures concerning how theories are evaluated; and how the discipline in question is related to the scientific community. We might say that the first matter is the outcome of the latter ones: if psychoanalysis became more closely related to universities and topical scientific debates—and only this way—its theories became more critically evaluated as well as enriched by the findings of other disciplines. The book at hand should also be seen that way: my aim has been to update the connection between psychoanalytic ideas and the grand themes of (behavioural) sciences.

REFERENCES

Aizava, K. & Gillett, C. (2009). The (multiple) realization of psychological and other properties in the sciences. *Mind & Language, 24*: 181–208.

Akhtar, S. (2009). *Comprehensive Dictionary of Psychoanalysis*. London: Karnac.

Andreasen, N. (2001). *Brave New Brain: Conquering Mental Illnesses in the Era of the Genome*. New York: Oxford University Press.

Audi, R. (1998). *Epistemology: A Contemporary Introduction to the Theory of Knowledge*. London: Routledge.

Bargh, J. (2005). Bypassing the will: Toward demystifying the nonconscious control of social behavior. In: R. Hassin, J. Uleman & J. Bargh (Eds.), *The New Unconscious* (pp. 37–58). Oxford: Oxford University Press.

Bechtel, W. (2005). Mental mechanisms: What are the operations? *Proceedings of the 27th Annual Meeting of the Cognitive Science Society*: 208–213. www.psych.unito.it/csc/cogsci05/frame/talk/f695-bechtel.pdf. [Last accessed 21 November 2011.]

Bechtel, W. (2007). Reducing psychology while maintaining its autonomy via mechanistic explanations. In: M. Schouten & H. Looren de Jong (Eds.), *The Matter of Mind: Philosophical Essays on Psychology, Neuroscience, and Reductionism* (pp. 172–198). Malden: Blackwell Publishing.

Bechtel, W. (2008). *Mental Mechanisms: Philosophical Perspectives on Cognitive Neuroscience*. London: Routledge.

Bechtel, W. & Abrahamsen, A. (2005). From reduction back to higher levels. *Studies in History and Philosophy of Science Part C: Studies in History and Philosophy of Biological and Biomedical Sciences, 36*: 421–441.

Bechtel, W. & Wright, C. (2009). What is psychological explanation? In: P. Calvo & J. Symons (Eds.), *Routledge Companion to Philosophy of Psychology* (pp. 113–130). London: Routledge. Available online at: http://mechanism.ucsd.edu/~bill/research/What%20is%20Psychological%20Explanation.web.pdf. [Last accessed 21 November 2011.]

Bem, S. (2001). The explanatory autonomy of psychology. *Theory & Psychology, 11*: 785–795.

Bem, S. & Looren de Jong, H. (2006). *Theoretical Issues in Psychology: An Introduction* (2nd edn). Los Angeles: Sage.

Bennett, M. R. & Hacker, P. M. S. (2003). *Philosophical Foundations of Neuroscience*. Malden: Blackwell Publishing.

Bermúdez, J. L. (2005). *Philosophy of Psychology: A Contemporary Introduction*. New York: Routledge.

Bickle, J. (2003). *Philosophy of Neuroscience: A Ruthless Reductive Account*. Dordrecht: Kluwer Academic Publishers.

Billig, M. (1999). *Freudian Repression: Conversation Creating the Unconscious*. Cambridge: Cambridge University Press.

Boag, S. (2011). "Verbal Magic" & the Five-Factor Model, *Philosophical Psychology, 24*: 223–243.

Bollas, C. (1995). *Cracking up: The Work of Unconscious Experience*. London: Routledge.

Bolton, D. & Hill, J. (2003). *Mind, Meaning, and Mental Disorder: The Nature of Causal Explanation in Psychology and Psychiatry* (2nd edn). Oxford: Oxford University Press.

Booth, W. (1961). *The Rhetoric of Fiction*. Chicago: University of Chicago Press.

Bouveresse, J. (1996). *Wittgenstein Reads Freud: The Myth of the Unconscious*. Carol Cosman (Trans.). Princeton: Princeton University Press.

Brakel, L. A. (1997). Commentaries. *Journal of the American Psychoanalytic Association, 45*: 714–720.

Brentano, F. (1973 [1874]). *Psychology from an Empirical Standpoint*. A. C. Rancurello, D. B. Terrell & L. McAlister (Trans.). London: Routledge.

Cambell, J. (2008). Causation in psychiatry. In: K. S. Kendler & J. Parnas (Eds.), *Philosophical Issues in Psychiatry* (pp. 196–235). Baltimore: The Johns Hopkins University Press.

Caprara, G. & Cervone, D. (2000). *Personality: Deteminants, Dynamics, and Potentials*. Cambridge: Cambridge University Press.

Carnap, R. (1995). *An Introduction to the Philosophy of Science*. M. Gardner (Ed.). New York: Dover Publications.

Chalmers, A. F. (1999). *What is This Thing Called Science?* (3rd edn). Glasgow: Bell & Bain.

Charter, N. & Oaksford, M. (1996). The falsifity of folk theories: Implications for psychology and philosophy. In: W. O'Donohue & R. Kitchener (Eds.), *The Philosophy of Psychology* (pp. 244–256). London: Sage Publications.

Chatman, S. (1978). *Story and Discourse: Narrative Structure in Fiction and Film*. New York: Cornell University Press.

Cooper, M. (2008). *Essential Research Findings in Counselling and Psychotherapy: The Facts are Friendly*. London: Sage.

Cooper, R. (2007). *Psychiatry and Philosophy of Science*. Stocksfield: Acumen.

Cottingham, J. (1992). Cartesian dualism: Theology, metaphysics, and science. In: J. Cottingham (Ed.), *The Cambridge Companion to Descartes* (pp. 236–257). Cambridge: Cambridge University Press.

Craver, C. F. (2007). *Explaining the Brain: Mechanisms and the Mosaic Unity of Neuroscience*. Oxford: Clarendon Press.

Cummins, R. (1983). *The Nature of Psychological Explanation*. Cambridge: The MIT Press.

Cummins, R. (2000). "How does it work?" vs. "What are the laws?": Two conceptions of psychological explanation. In: F. Keil & R. Wilson (Eds.), *Explanation and Cognition* (pp. 118–144). Cambridge: The MIT Press.

Davies, J. (2009). *The Making of Psychotherapists: An Anthropological Analysis*. London: Karnac.

Dennett, D. (1987). *The Intentional Stance*. Cambridge: MIT Press.

Dennett, D. (1991). *Consciousness Explained*. Boston: Little, Brown & Co.

Dretske, F. (1997). *Naturalizing the Mind*. Cambridge: A Bradford Book.

Edelman, G. M. & Tononi, G. (2000). *Consciousness: How Matter Becomes Imagination*. London: Penguin Press.

Elster, J. (1989). *Nuts and Bolts for the Social Sciences*. Cambridge: Cambridge University Press.

Elster, J. (1998). A plea for mechanisms. In: P. Hedström & R. Swedberg (Eds.), *Social Mechanisms: An Analytical Approach to Social Theory* (pp. 45–73). Cambridge: Cambridge University Press.

Erwin, E. (1988). Psychoanalysis: Clinical versus experimental evidence. In P. Clark & C. Wright (Eds.), *Mind, Psychoanalysis and Science* (pp. 205–223). Cambridge: Basil Blackwell.

Erwin, E. (1996). *A Final Account: Philosophical and Empirical Issues in Freudian Psychology*. Cambridge: The MIT Press.

Erwin, E. (1997). *Philosophy & Psychotherapy: Razing the Troubles of the Brain*. London: SAGE Publications.

Erwin, E. (2010). *The Rejection of Natural Science Approaches to Psychotherapy: Philosophical Issues*. Saarbrücken: VDM Verlag Dr. Müller.

Fichtner, G. (Ed.) (1992). *Sigmund Freud—Ludwig Binswanger Correspondence*. New York: Other Press.

Fodor, J. (1989). Making mind matter more. *Philosophical Topics, 17*: 59–79.

Fonagy, P., Gergely, G., Jurist, E. & Target, M. (2002). *Affect Regulation, Mentalization, and the Development of the Self*. London: Karnac.

Freud, S. (1891). *Zur Auffassung der Aphasien: Eine kritische Studie* [*On Aphasia: A Critical Study*]. Vienna: Franz Deuticke.

Freud, S. (1894). The neuro-psychoses of defence. *The Standard Edition, 3*: 43–61.

Freud, S. (1950 [1895]). Project for a scientific psychology. *The Standard Edition of the Complete Psychological Works, 1*: 281–391.

Freud, S. (1896). Further remarks on the neuro-psychoses of defence. *The Standard Edition, 3*: 162–185.

Freud, S. (1898a). Sexuality in the aetiology of the neuroses. *The Standard Edition, 3*: 261–285.

Freud, S. (1898b). The psychical mechanism of forgetfulness. *The Standard Edition, 3*: 287–297.

Freud, S. (1900). The interpretation of dreams. *The Standard Edition*, 4/5.

Freud, S. (1915). The unconscious. *The Standard Edition, 14*: 161–215.

Freud, S. (1923a). Two encyclopaedia articles. *The Standard Edition, 18*: 233–260.

Freud, S. (1923b). The ego and the id. *The Standard Edition, 19*: 3–66.

Freud, S. (1926). Inhibitions, symptoms, and anxiety. *The Standard Edition, 20*: 77–174.

Freud, S. (1933). New introductory lectures on psycho-analysis. *The Standard Edition, 22*: 3–182.

Freud, A. (1966 [1936]). *The Ego and the Mechanisms of Defence*. New York: International Universities Press.

Freud, S. & Breuer, J. (1893). On the psychical mechanism of hysterical phenomena: Preliminary communication. *The Standard Edition, 2*: 1–7.

Frosh, S. (1997). *For and Against Psychoanalysis*. London: Routledge.

Fulgencio, L. (2000). Apresentação e Comentário do Documento Convocação para a Fundação de Uma "Sociedade para a Filosofia Positivista" [Presentation of and commentary on the document "A call for the foundation of a Society for Positivist Philosophy"]. *Natureza Humana, Revista Internacional de Filosofia e Práticas Psicoterápicas, 2*: 429–438.

Fulgencio, L. (2005). Freud's metapsychological speculations. *The International Journal of Psychoanalysis, 86*: 99–123.

Galdston, I. (1956). Freud and romantic medicine. *Bulletin of the History of Medicine, 30*: 489–507.

Gay, P. (1988). *Freud: A Life for Our Time*. New York: W. W. Norton.

Godfrey-Smith, P. (2003). *Theory and Reality: An Introduction to the Philosophy of Science*. Chicago: The University of Chicago Press.

Gomez, L. (2005). *The Freud Wars: An Introduction to the Philosophy of Psychoanalysis*. London: Routledge.

Grosskurth, P. (1991). *The Secret Ring: Freud's Inner Circle and the Politics of Psychoanalysis*. New York: Addison Wesley.

Grünbaum, A. (1993). *Validation in the Clinical Theory of Psychoanalysis: A Study in the Philosophy of Psychoanalysis*. Madison: International Universities Press.

Grünbaum, A. (2004). The hermeneutic versus the scientific conception of psychoanalysis. In: J. Mills (Ed.), *Psychoanalysis at the Limit: Epistemology, Mind, and the Question of Science* (pp. 139–160). New York: State University of New York Press.

Hacker, P. E. M. (2010). *Human Nature: The Categorical Framework*. Oxford: Wiley-Blackwell.

Haldane, J. (1988). Psychoanalysis, cognitive psychology and self-consciousness. In: P. Clark & C. Wright (Eds.), *Mind, Psychoanalysis and Science* (pp. 113–139). Oxford: Basil Blackwell.

Hassin, R. R., Uleman, J. S. & Bargh, J. A. (Eds.) (2005). *The New Unconscious*. Oxford: Oxford University Press.

Hatfield, G. (1992). Descartes' physiology and its relation to his psychology. In: J. Cottingham (Ed.), *The Cambridge Companion to Descartes* (pp. 335–370). Cambridge: Cambridge University Press.

Hedström, P. (2009). Studying mechanisms to strengthen causal inferences in quantitative research. In: J. Box-Steffensmeier & D. Collier (Eds.), *The Oxford Handbook of Political Methodology* (pp. 319–335). Oxford: Oxford University Press. http://www.nuffield.ox.ac.uk/users/hedstrom/inference.pdf. [Last accessed 21 November 2011.]

Hempel, C. G. (1966). *Philosophy of Natural Science*. NJ: Prentice-Hall. Reprinted in: Schik, T. (Ed.) (2000) *Readings in the Philosophy of Science: From Positivism to Postmodernism*. London: Mayfield Publishing Company.

Karlsson, G. (2010). *Psychoanalysis in a New Light*. Cambridge: Cambridge University Press.

Kendler, K. S. & Parnas, J. (Eds.) (2008). *Philosophical Issues in Psychiatry: Explanation, Phenomenology, and Nosology*. Baltimore: The Johns Hopkins University Press.

Kernberg, O. (2011). Psychoanalysis and the university: A difficult relationship. *The International Journal of Psychoanalysis, 92*: 609–622.

Kim, J. (1998). *Philosophy of Mind*. Colorado: Westview Press.

Kim, J. (2005). *Physicalism, Or Something Near Enough*. Princeton: Princeton University Press.

Kim, J. (2010). *Essays in the Metaphysics of Mind*. Oxford: Oxford University Press.

Kitcher, P. (1992). *Freud's Dream: A Complete Interdisciplinary Science of Mind*. London: The MIT Press.

Koons, R. & Bealer, G. (Eds.) (2010). *The Waning of Materialism*. Oxford: Oxford University Press.

Lagache, D. (1973). Introduction. In: J. Laplanche & J.-P. Pontalis (Eds.), *The Language of Psychoanalysis* (pp. vii–ix). Donald Nicholson-Smith (Trans.). London: Karnac.

Latour, B. & Woolgar, S. (1979). *Laboratory Life: The Social Construction of Scientific Facts*. Beverly Hills: Sage.

LeDoux, J. (1998). *The Emotional Brain: The Mysterious Underpinnings of Emotional Life*. London: Phoenix.

Leicester, H. (1956). *The Historical Background of Chemistry*. New York: Dover Publications.

Lennon, K. (1990). *Explaining Human Action*. La Salle: Open Court Publishing Company.

Loewenstein, E. (1992). The Freudian case history: A detective story or a dialectical progression? Reflections on psychoanalytic narratives from a Lacanian perspective. *Psychoanalytic Psychology, 9*: 49–59.

Looren de Jong, H. & Schouten, M. (2007). Mind reading and mirror neurons: Exploring reduction. In: M. Schouten & H. Looren de Jong (Eds.), *The Matter of Mind: Philosophical Essays on Psychology, Neuroscience, and Reductionism* (pp. 298–322). Malden: Blackwell Publishing.

Loux, M. J. (2006). *Metaphysics: A Contemporary Introduction* (3rd edn). New York: Routledge.

Machamer, P., Darden, L. & Craver, C. (2000). Thinking about mechanisms. *Philosophy of Science, 67*: 1–25.

Machamer, P. & Sytsma, J. (2007). Neuroscience and theoretical psychology—what's to worry about? *Theory & Psychology, 17*: 199–216.

MacIntyre, A. (1958). *The Unconscious: A Conceptual Analysis*. London: Routledge & Kegan Paul.

Mackie, J. L. (1965). Causes and conditions. *American Philosophical Quarterly, 2*: 245–264. Reprinted in: Loux, M. (Ed.) (2008). *Metaphysics: Contemporary Readings* (2nd edn). New York: Routledge.

Mahoney, J. (2003). Tentative answers to question about causal mechanisms. *Presentation in the Meeting of the American Political Science Association 28.8*.

Masson, J. M. (Ed.) (1985). *The Complete Letters of Sigmund Freud to Wilhelm Fliess, 1887–1904*. Cambridge: The Belknap Press of Harvard University Press.

Mayr, E. (1997). *This is Biology: The Science of the Living World*. Cambridge: The Belknap Press of Harvard University Press.

McAdams, D. (1992). The Five-Factor Model in personality: A critical appraisal. *Journal of Personality*, 2: 329–361.

Mele, A. R. (2001). *Self-deception Unmasked*. Princeton: Princeton University Press.

Miller, G. A. (1956). The magical number seven, plus or minus two: some limits on our capacity for processing information. *Psychological Review*, *63*: 81–97.

Minsky, M. (1988). *The Society of Mind*. New York: Simon & Schuster.

Mitchell, S. D. (2008). Explaining complex behavior. In: K. S. Kendler & J. Parnas (Eds.), *Philosophical Issues in Psychiatry: Explanation, Phenomenology, and Nosology* (pp. 19–38). Baltimore: The Johns Hopkins University Press.

Modell, A. (2003). *Imagination and the Meaningful Brain*. Cambridge: The MIT Press.

Murphy, D. (2006). *Psychiatry in the Scientific Image*. Cambridge: The MIT Press.

Murphy, D. P. (2008). Levels of explanation in psychiatry. In: K. S. Kendler & J. Parnas (Eds.), *Philosophical Issues in Psychiatry: Explanation, Phenomenology, and Nosology* (pp. 99–125). Baltimore: The Johns Hopkins University Press.

Nisbett, R. E. & Ross, L. D. (1980). *Human Inference: Strategies and Shortcomings of Social Judgment*. Englewood Cliffs: Prentice-Hall.

Northoff, G. & Boeker, H. (2006). Principles of neuronal integration and defence mechanisms: Neuropsychoanalytic hypothesis. *Neuro-Psychoanalysis*, *8*: 69–84.

O'Brien, G. & Jureidini, J. (2002). Dispensing with the dynamic unconscious. *Philosophy, Psychology, and Psychiatry*, *9*: 141–153.

Ogden, T. (1997). *Reverie and Interpretation: Sensing Something Human*. London: Karnac.

Oppenheim, L. (2005). *A Curious Intimacy: Art and Neuro-psychoanalysis*. London: Routledge.

Paris, J. (2005). *The Fall of an Icon: Psychoanalysis and Academic Psychiatry*. Toronto: University of Toronto Press.

Paris, J. (2008). *Prescriptions for the Mind: A Critical View of Contemporary Psychiatry*. Oxford: Oxford University Press.

Peräkylä. A. (2005). Patients' responses to interpretations: A dialogue between conversation analysis and psychoanalytic theory. *Communication & Medicine*, 2: 163–176.

Peräkylä, A. (2010). Shifting the perspective after the patient's response to an interpretation. *The International Journal of Psychoanalysis*, *96*: 1,363–1,384.

Peressini, A. (1997). Psychological explanation and behavior broadly conceived. *Behavior and Philosophy*, *25*: 137–159.

Place, U. T. (1996). Folk psychology from the standpoint of conceptual analysis. In: W. O'Donohue & R. Kitchener (Eds.), *The Philosophy of Psychology*, (pp. 264–270). London: Sage Publications.

Pockett, S., Banks, W. & Gallagher, S. (Eds.) (2006). *Does Consciousness Cause Behavior?* Cambridge: The MIT Press.

Reeder, J. (2004). *Hate and Love in Psychoanalytical Institutions: The Dilemma of a Profession*. New York: Other Press.

Richard, G. (1996). On the necessary survival of folk psychology. In: W. O'Donohue & R. Kitchener (Eds.), *The Philosophy of Psychology* (pp. 270–275). London: Sage Publications.

Robertson, L. C. (2003). Binding, spatial attention, and perceptual awareness. *Nature Reviews Neuroscience*, *4*: 92–103. http://socrates.berkeley.edu/~lynnlab/pubs/NatRevNeurosci03.pdf. [Last accessed 21 November 2011.]

Rofé, Y. (2008). Does repression exist? Memory, pathogenic, unconscious and clinical evidence. *Review of General Psychology*, *12*: 63–85.

Rosenberg, A. (2000). *Philosophy of Science: A Contemporary Introduction* (2nd edn). New York: Routledge.

Rubinstein, B. B. (1997). *Psychoanalysis and the Philosophy of Science: Collected Papers of Benjamin B. Rubinstein*. R. R. Holt (Ed.). Madison: International Universities Press.

Sandler, J. (1983). Reflections on some relations between psychoanalytic concepts and psychoanalytic practise. *The International Journal of Psychoanalysis*, *64*: 35–45.

Schaffner, K. F. (2008). Etiological models in psychiatry: Reductive and nonreductive approaches. In: K. S. Kendler & J. Parnas (Eds.), *Philosophical Issues in Psychiatry: Explanation, Phenomenology, and Nosology* (pp. 48–90). Baltimore: The Johns Hopkins University Press.

Schmidt-Hellerau, C. (1995). *Life Drive & Death Drive, Libido & Lethe: A Formalized Consistent Model of Psychoanalytic Drive and Structure Theory*. P. Slotkin (Trans.). New York: Other Press.

Schouten, M. & Looren de Jong, L. (Eds.) (2007). *The Matter of Mind: Philosophical Essays on Psychology, Neuroscience, and Reductionism*. Malden: Blackwell Publishing.

Searle, J. (1992). *The Rediscovery of the Mind*. Cambridge: The MIT Press.

Searle, J. (2008). *Philosophy in a New Centrury: Selected Essays*. Cambridge: Cambridge University Press.

Sharpe, R. (1988). Mirros, lamps, organisms, and texts. In: P. Clark & C. Wright (Eds.), *Mind, Psychoanalysis and Science* (pp. 187–201). Oxford: Basil Blackwell.

Shedler, J. (2010). The efficacy of psychodynamic psychotherapy. *American Psychologist, 63*: 98–109.

Slife, B. (2004). Theoretical challenges to therapy practise and research: The constraint of naturalism. In: M. J. Lambert (Ed.), *Bergin and Garfield's Handbook of Psychotherapy and Behavior Change* (5th edn) (pp. 44–83). New York: Wiley.

Smith, B. (1996). Does science underwrite our folk psychology? In: W. O'Donohue & R. Kitchener (Eds.), *The Philosophy of Psychology*, (pp. 256–264). London: Sage Publications.

Smith, D. L. (1999). Sigmund Freud's programme for a science of consciousness. *British Journal of Psychotherapy, 15*: 412–424.

Smith, K. (2009). Psychotherapy as applied science or moral praxis: The limitations of empirically supported treatment. *Journal of Theoretical and Philosophical Psychology, 29*: 34–46.

Smith, R. J. (2010). Against treating introspection as perception-like. *Psyche, 16(1)*: 79–86. www.theassc.org/vol_16_no_1_2010.

Solms, M. (1997). What is consciousness? *Journal of the American Psychoanalytic Association, 45*: 681–703.

Sonnenberg, S. (2011). Psychoanalysis and the United States research university: Current trends. *The International Journal of Psychoanalysis, 92*: 641–659.

Squire, L. & Kandel, E. (1999). *Memory: From Mind to Molecules*. New York: Scientific American Library.

Stanovich, K. (2010). *How to Think Straight about Psychology* (9th edn). Boston: Pearson.

Stalnaker, R. S. (2008). *Our Knowledge of the Internal World*. New York: Oxford University Press.

Stepansky, P. (2009). *Psychoanalysis at the Margins*. New York: Other Press.

Strawson, G. (1994). *Mental Reality*. Cambridge: The MIT Press.

Sulloway, F. J. (1979). *Freud, Biologist of the Mind: Beyond the Psychoanalytic Legend*. New York: Basic Books.

Talvitie, V. (2009). *The Freudian Unconscious and Cognitive Neuroscience: From Unconscious Fantasies to Neural Algorithms*. London: Karnac.

Talvitie, V. & Ihanus, J. (2002). The repressed and implicit knowledge. *The International Journal of Psychoanalysis, 83*: 1,311–1,323.

Talvitie, V. & Ihanus, J. (2006). The psychic apparatus, metapsychology and neuroscience—Toward biological (neuro) psychoanalysis. *Neuro-Psychoanalysis, 8*: 85–98.

Talvitie, V. & Ihanus, J. (2011a). On the relation between neural and psychological mechanisms—neuropsychoanalysis and the "new mechanists". *The Scandinavian Psychoanalytic Review, 33*: 130–141.

Talvitie, V. & Ihanus, J. (2011b). On neuropsychoanalytic metaphysics. *The International Journal of Psychoanalysis.*

Talvitie, V. & Tiitinen, H. (2006). From the repression of contents to the rules of the (narrative) self: A present-day cognitive view to "The Freudian phenomenon" of repressed contents. *Psychology & Psychotherapy: Theory, Research and Practise, 79*: 165–181.

Tauber, A. (2010). *Freud, the Reluctant Philosopher*. Princeton: Princeton University Press.

Taylor, C. (1986 [1971]). Interpretation and the sciences of man. *The Review of Metaphysics, 25*: 3–51. Reprinted in: *Philosophy and the Human Sciences: Philosophical Papers*. Cambridge: Cambridge University Press.

Taylor, C. (1985). Introduction. In: *Human Agency and Language: Philosophical Papers 1* (pp. 1–12). Cambridge: Cambridge University Press.

Thompson, M. (2004). The role of being and experience in Freud's unconscious ontology. In: J. Mills (Ed.), *Psychoanalysis at the Limit* (pp. 1–30). Albany: State University of New York Press.

Uleman, J. S. (2005). Introduction. In: R. R. Hassin, J. S. Uleman & J. A. Bargh (Eds.), *The New Unconscious* (pp. 3–15). Oxford: Oxford University Press.

Valentine, E. (1992). *Conceptual Issues in Psychology*. London: Routledge.

Valentine, E. (1996). Folk psychology and its implications for cognitive science. In: W. O'Donohue & R. Kitchener (Eds.), *The Philosophy of Psychology* (pp. 275–278). London: Sage Publications.

van Fraassen, B. (2008). *Scientific Representation: Paradoxes of Perspective*. New York: Oxford University Press.

Vehviläinen, S. (2003). Preparing and delivering interpretations in psychoanalytic interaction. *Text, 23*: 573–606.

Volkan, V. (1987). *Six Steps in the Treatment of Borderline Personality Organization*. Northvale: Jason Aronson.

Waelder, R. (2007). The principle of multiple function: Observations on over-determination. *Psychoanalytic Quarterly, 76*: 75–92.

Wallerstein, R. (2011). Psychoanalysis in the university: The natural home for education and research. *The International Journal of Psychoanalysis, 92*: 623–639.

Watt, D. F. (2003). Psychotherapy in an age of neuroscience: Bridges to affective neuroscience. In: J. Corrigall & H. Wilkinson (Eds.), *Revolutionary Connections: Psychotherapy and Neuroscience*. (pp. 79–115). London: Karnac.

Westen, D. (1998). The scientific legacy of Sigmund Freud: Toward a psychodynamically informed psychological science. *Psychological Bulletin, 124*: 333–371.

Wimsatt, W. (2007). *Re-engineering Philosophy for Limited Beings: Piecewise Approximations to Reality*. Cambridge: Harvard University Press.

Wittgenstein, L. (1953 [2001]). *Philosophical Investigations*. Oxford: Blackwell Publishing.

Wittgenstein, L. (1961 [1922]). *Tractatus Logico-Philosophicus [Logical-Philosophical Treatise]*. D. F. Pears & B. F. McGuinness (Trans.). London: Routledge and Kegan Paul.

Woodward, J. F. (2008). Cause and explanation in psychiatry: An interventionist perspective. In: K. S. Kendler & J. Parnas (Eds.), *Philosophical Issues in Psychiatry* (pp. 132–195). Baltimore: The Johns Hopkins University Press.

Wright, C. & Bechtel, W. (2007). Mechanisms and psychological explanation. In: P. Thagard (Ed.), *Philosophy of Psychology and Cognitive Science* (Volume 4 of *The Handbook of the Philosophy of Science*) (pp. 31–79). New York: Elsevier. http://mechanism.ucsd.edu/~bill/research/mechanismsandpsychexplanation.pdf. [Last accessed 21 November 2011.]

Yu, C. K. (2003). Neuroanatomical correlates of dreaming III: The frontal-lobe controversy (dream censorship). *Neuro-Psychoanalysis, 5*: 159–169.

Zachar, P. (2000). *Psychological Concepts and Biological Psychiatry: A Philosophical Analysis*. Amsterdam: John Benjamins.

INDEX